Globalization

WITHDRAWN

THEMES FOR THE 21ST CENTURY

Titles in this series

Globalization

The Human Consequences

ZYGMUNT BAUMAN

Polity

First published in 1998 by Polity Press
in association with Blackwell Publishers Ltd.
Reprinted 1999 (twice), 2000 (twice), 2005, 2006, 2007

Polity Press
65 Bridge Street
Cambridge CB2 1UR, UK

ISBN 978-0-7456-2012-1
ISBN 978-0-7456-2013-8 (pb)

A catalogue record for this book is available from the British Library.

Typeset in 10.5 on 12 pt Plantin
by SetSystems Ltd, Saffron Walden, Essex
Printed in Great Britain by TJ International Ltd, Padstow

This book is printed on acid-free paper

Contents

Introduction

'Globalization' is on everybody's lips; a fad word fast turning into a shibboleth, a magic incantation, a pass-key meant to unlock the gates to all present and future mysteries. For some, 'globalization' is what we are bound to do if we wish to be happy; for others 'globalization' is the cause of our unhappiness. For everybody, though, 'globalization' is the intractable fate of the world, an irreversible process; it is also a process which affects us all in the same measure and in the same way. We are all being 'globalized' – and being 'globalized' means much the same to all who 'globalized' are.

All vogue words tend to share a similar fate: the more experiences they pretend to make transparent, the more they themselves become opaque. The more numerous are the ortho-dox truths they elbow out and supplant, the faster they turn into no-questions-asked canons. Such human practices as the concept tried originally to grasp recede from view, and it is now the 'facts of the matter', the quality of 'the world out there' which the term seems to 'get straight' and which it invokes to claim its own immunity to questioning. 'Globalization' is no exception to that rule.

This book is an attempt to show that there is more to the phenomenon of globalization than meets the eye; unpacking the social roots and social consequences of the globalizing process, it will try to disperse some of the mist which surrounds the term that claims to bring clarity to the present-day human condition.

The term 'time/space compression' encapsulates the ongoing multi-faceted transformation of the parameters of the human condition. Once the social causes and outcomes of that compression are looked into, it will become evident that the globalizing processes lack the commonly assumed unity of effects. The uses of time and space are sharply differentiated as well as differentiating. Globalization divides as much as it unites; it divides as it unites – the causes of division being identical with those which promote the uniformity of the globe. Alongside the emerging planetary dimensions of business, finance, trade and information flow, a 'localizing', space-fixing process is set in motion. Between them, the two closely inter-connected processes sharply differentiate the existential conditions of whole populations and of various segments of each one of the populations. What appears as globalization for some means localization for others; signalling a new freedom for some, upon many others it descends as an uninvited and cruel fate. Mobility climbs to the rank of the uppermost among the coveted values – and the freedom to move, perpetually a scarce and unequally distributed commodity, fast becomes the main stratifying factor of our late-modern or postmodern times.

All of us are, willy-nilly, by design or by default, on the move. We are on the move even if, physically, we stay put: immobility is not a realistic option in a world of permanent change. And yet the effects of that new condition are radically unequal. Some of us become fully and truly 'global'; some are fixed in their 'locality' – a predicament neither pleasurable nor endurable in the world in which the 'globals' set the tone and compose the rules of the life-game.

Being local in a globalized world is a sign of social deprivation and degradation. The discomforts of localized existence are compounded by the fact that with public spaces removed beyond the reaches of localized life, localities are losing their meaning-generating and meaning-negotiating capacity and are increasingly dependent on sense-giving and interpreting actions which they do not control – so much for the communitarianist dreams/consolations of the globalized intellectuals.

An integral part of the globalizing processes is progressive spatial segregation, separation and exclusion. Neo-tribal and fundamentalist tendencies, which reflect and articulate the experience of people on the receiving end of globalization, are as much legitimate offspring of globalization as the widely acclaimed 'hybridization' of top culture – the culture at the globalized top. A particular cause for worry is the progressive breakdown in communication between the increasingly global and extraterritorial elites and the ever more 'localized' rest. The centres of meaning-and-value production are today exterritorial and emancipated from local constraints – this does not apply, though, to the human condition which such values and meanings are to inform and make sense of.

With the freedom of mobility at its centre, the present-day polarization has many dimensions; the new centre puts a new gloss on the time-honoured distinctions between rich and poor, the nomads and the settled, the 'normal' and the abnormal or those in breach of law. Just how these various dimensions of polarity intertwine and influence each other is another complex problem this book attempts to unpack.

The first chapter considers the link between the historically changing nature of time and space and the pattern and scale of social organization – and particularly the effects of the present-day time/space compression on the structuration of planetary and territorial societies and communities. One of the effects scrutinized is the new version of 'absentee landlordship' – the newly acquired independence of global elites from territorially confined units of political and cultural power, and the consequent 'disempowerment' of the latter. The impact of the separation between the two settings in which the 'top' and the 'bottom' of the new hierarchy are respectively located is traced to the changing organization of space and the changing meaning of 'neighbourhood' in the contemporary metropolis.

The successive stages of modern wars for the right to define and enforce the meaning of shared space is the subject of the second chapter. The past adventures of comprehensive town planning, as well as the contemporary tendencies to fragmentation of design and to building for exclusion, are analysed in this light. Finally, the historical fate of Panopticon as the once favourite modern pattern of social control, and particularly its present irrelevance and gradual demise, are scrutinized.

The topic of the third chapter is the prospects of political sovereignty – and particularly of the self-constitution and self-government of national, and more generally territorial, communities, under conditions of globalized economy, finance and information. At the centre of attention is the widening discrepancy of scale between the realm of institutionalized decision-making and the universe in which the resources necessary for decisions and their implementation are produced, distributed, appropriated and deployed; in particular, the disabling effects of globalization on the decision-making capacity of the state governments – the major, and still unreplaced foci of effective social management for the greater part of modern history.

The fourth chapter takes stock of the cultural consequences of the above transformations. Their overall effect, it is postulated, is the bifurcation and polarization of human experience, with shared cultural tokens serving two sharply distinct interpretations. 'Being on the move' has a radically different, opposite sense for, respectively, those at the top and those at the bottom of the new hierarchy; with the bulk of the population – the 'new middle class', oscillating between the two extremes – bearing the brunt of that opposition and suffering acute existential uncertainty, anxiety and fear as a result. It is argued that the need to mitigate such fears and neutralize the potential of the discontent they contain is in its own turn a powerful factor in the further polarization of the two meanings of mobility.

The last chapter explores the extremal expressions of that polarization: the present-day tendency to criminalize cases falling below the idealized norm, and the role played by criminalization in offsetting the discomforts of 'life on the move' by rendering the image and the reality of alternative life, the life of immobility, ever more odious and repelling. The complex issue of existential insecurity brought about by the process of globalization tends to be reduced to the apparently straightforward issue of 'law and order'. On the way, concerns with 'safety', more often than not trimmed down to the single-issue worry about the safety of the body and personal possessions, are 'overloaded', by being charged with anxieties generated by other, crucial dimensions of present-day existence – insecurity and uncertainty.

The theses of the book do not amount to a policy statement. In the intention of its author it is a discussion paper. Many more questions are asked here than answered, and no coherent forecast of the future consequences of present-day trends is arrived at. And yet – as Cornelius Castoriadis put it – the trouble with the contemporary condition of our modern civilization is that it stopped questioning itself. Not asking certain questions is pregnant with more dangers than failing to answer the questions already on the official agenda; while asking the wrong kind of questions all too often helps to avert eyes from the truly important issues. The price of silence is paid in the hard currency of human suffering. Asking the right questions makes, after all, all the difference between fate and destination, drifting and travelling. Questioning the ostensibly unquestionable premises of our way of life is arguably the most urgent of the services we owe our fellow humans and ourselves. This book is first and foremost an exercise in asking and prompting the asking of questions – without the pretence that it is asking the right questions, all the right questions, and, most important, all the questions that have been asked.

1

Time and Class

'The company belongs to people who invest in it – not to its employees, suppliers, nor the locality in which it is situated.'[1] This is how Albert J. Dunlap, the celebrated 'rationalizer' of modern enterprise (a *dépeceur* – 'chopper', 'quarterer', 'dismemberer' – in the juicy yet precise designation of the CNRS sociologist Denis Duclos)[2] summarized his creed in the self-congratulating report of his activities which Times Books published for the enlightenment and edification of all seekers of economic progress.

What Dunlap had in mind was not, of course, the simple question of 'belonging' as just another name for the purely legal issue of ownership, an issue hardly contested and even less in need of restating – let alone such an emphatic restating. What Dunlap had in mind was, mostly, what the rest of the sentence implied: that the employees, the suppliers and the spokesmen of the community have no say in the decisions that the 'people who invest' may take; and that the true decision-makers, the investors, have the right to dismiss out of hand, and to declare irrelevant and invalid, any postulates which such people may make concerning the way they run the company.

Let us note: Dunlap's message is not a declaration of intent, but a statement of fact. Dunlap takes it for granted that the principle it conveys has passed all the tests which economic, political, social and any other realities of our times might have set or make proper to examine its viability. It has by now entered the family of self-evident truths which serve to explain the world while themselves needing no explanation; which help to assert things about the world while themselves no longer being seen as assertions, let alone contentious and arguable assertions.

There were times (one would say 'not so long ago', if not for the fast shrinking span of collective attention, which makes even a week not just a long time in politics, but an exceedingly long stretch in the life of human memory) when Dunlap's proclamation would have seemed by no means obvious to all; when it would have sounded more like a war-cry or a battlefield report. In the early years of Margaret Thatcher's war of annihilation launched against local self-government, businessman after businessman felt the need to climb rostrums of the Tory Annual Conference to hammer out again and again a message they must have thought to be in need of hammering out because of sounding uncanny and bizarre to yet untuned ears: the message that companies would gladly pay local taxes to support road building or sewage repairs which they needed, but that they saw no reason to pay for the support of the local unemployed, invalids and other human waste, for whose fate they did not feel like carrying a responsibility or assuming an obligation. But those were the early years of the war which has been all but won a mere two dozen years later, at the time Dunlap dictated his credo, which he could rightly expect every listener to share.

There is not much point in debating whether that war was malevolently and surreptitiously plotted in smoke-free company boardrooms, or whether the necessity of war action was visited on unsuspecting, peace-loving leaders of industry by changes brought about by a mixture of the mysterious forces of new technology and the new global competitiveness; or whether it was a war planned in advance, duly declared and with its goals clearly defined, or just a series of scattered and often

unanticipated warlike actions, each necessitated by causes of its
own. Whichever of the two was the case (there are good
arguments to be advanced for each, but it may well be that the
two accounts only seem to be in competition with each other),
it is quite probable that the last quarter of the current century
will go down in history as the Great War of Independence from
Space. What happened in the course of that war was a consistent
and relentless wrenching of the decision-making centres,
together with the calculations which ground the decisions such
centres make, free from territorial constraints – the constraints
of locality.

Let us look more closely at Dunlap's principle. Employees
are recruited from the local population and – burdened as they
might be by family duties, home ownership and the like – could
not easily follow the company once it moves elsewhere. Suppliers have to deliver the supplies, and low transport costs give
the local suppliers an advantage which disappears once the
company changes its location. As to the 'locality' itself – it will,
obviously, stay where it is and can hardly change its location,
whatever the new address of the company. Among all the
named candidates who have a say in the running of a company,
only 'people who invest' – the shareholders – are in no way
space-tied; they can buy any share at any stock-exchange and
through any broker, and the geographical nearness or distance
of the company will be in all probability the least important
consideration in their decision to buy or sell.

In principle there is nothing space-determined in the disper-
sion of the shareholders. They are the sole factor genuinely
free from spatial determination. And it is to them, and to them
only, that the company 'belongs'. It is up to them therefore
to move the company wherever they spy out or anticipate a
chance of higher dividends, leaving to all others – locally bound
as they are – the task of wound-licking, damage-repair and
waste-disposal. The company is free to move; but the consequences of the move are bound to stay. Whoever is free to run

away from the locality, is free to run away from the consequences. These are the most important spoils of victorious
space war.

Absentee landlords, mark II

In the post-space-war world, mobility has become the most
powerful and most coveted stratifying factor; the stuff of which
the new, increasingly world-wide, social, political, economic
and cultural hierarchies are daily built and rebuilt. And to those
at the top of the new hierarchy freedom to move brings
advantages far beyond those short-listed in Dunlap's formula.
That formula takes note of, promotes or demotes only such
competitors who may make themselves audible – those who
can, and are likely to, voice their grievances and forge their
complaints into claims. But there are other – also locally bound,
cut-off and left-behind connections, on which Dunlap's formula
keeps silent because they are unlikely to make themselves heard.

The mobility acquired by 'people who invest' – those with
capital, with money which the investment requires – means the
new, indeed unprecedented in its radical unconditionality,
disconnection of power from obligations: duties towards
employees, but also towards the younger and weaker, towards
yet unborn generations and towards the self-reproduction of the
living conditions of all; in short, freedom from the duty to
contribute to daily life and the perpetuation of the community.
There is a new asymmetry emerging between exterritorial
nature of power and the continuing territoriality of the 'whole
life' – which the now unanchored power, able to move at short
notice or without warning, is free to exploit and abandon to the
consequences of that exploitation. Shedding the responsibility
for the consequences is the most coveted and cherished gain
which the new mobility brings to free-floating, locally unbound
capital. The costs of coping with the consequences need not be

now counted in the calculation of the 'effectiveness' of investment.

The new freedom of capital is reminiscent of that of the absentee landlords of yore, notorious for their much resented neglect of the needs of the populations which fed them. Creaming off the 'surplus product' was the sole interest the absentee landlords held in the existence of the land they owned. There is certainly some similarity here – but the comparison does not give full justice to the kind of freedom from worry and responsibility which the mobile capital of the late twentieth century acquired but the absentee landlords never could.

The latter could not exchange one land estate for another and so remained – however tenuously – tied to the locality from which they drew their life juices; that circumstance set a practical limit to the theoretically and legally unconstrained possibility of exploitation, lest the future flow of income might thin out or dry up completely. True, the real limits tended to be on the whole more severe than the perceived ones, and these in their turn were all too often more severe than the limits observed in practice – a circumstance which made absentee land-ownership prone to inflict irreparable damage upon soil fertility and agricultural proficiency in general, and which also made the fortunes of absentee landlords notoriously precarious, tending to decline over the generations. And yet there were genuine limits, which reminded of their presence all the more cruelly for being unperceived and not complied with. And a limit, as Alberto Melucci put it, 'stands for confinement, frontier, separation; it therefore also signifies recognition of the other, the different, the irreducible. The encounter with other-ness is an experience that puts us to a test: from it is born the temptation to reduce difference by force, while it may equally generate the challenge of communication, as a constantly renewed endeavour.'[3]

In contradistinction to the absentee landlords of early modern times, the late-modern capitalists and land-brokers, thanks to the new mobility of their by now liquid resources, do not face limits sufficiently real – solid, tough, resistant – to enforce compliance. The sole limits which could make themselves felt and respected would be those administratively imposed on the free movement of capital and money. Such limits are, however, few and far between, and the handful that remain are under tremendous pressure to be effaced or just washed out. In their absence there would be few occasions for Melucci's 'encounter with otherness'. If it so happened that the encounter were enforced by the other side – the moment 'otherness' tried to flex its muscles and make its strength felt, capital would have little difficulty with packing its tents and finding an environment that was more hospitable – that is, unresistant, malleable, soft. There would therefore be fewer occasions likely to prompt either attempts to 'reduce difference by force' or the will to accept 'the challenge of communication'.

Both attitudes would have implied recognition of the irreducibility of otherness, but, in order to be seen as irreducible, 'otherness' must first constitute itself into a resistant, inflexible, literally 'gripping', entity. Its chance to do so is, however, fast shrinking. To acquire a genuinely entity-constituting capacity the resistance needs a persistent and effective attacker – but the overall effect of the new mobility is that, for capital and finances, the need to bend the inflexible, to push the hurdles aside or to overcome or mitigate resistance hardly ever arises; if it does arise it may well be brushed aside in favour of a softer option. Capital can always move away to more peaceful sites if the engagement with 'otherness' requires a costly application of force or tiresome negotiations. No need to engage, if avoidance will do.

Freedom of movement and the self-constitution of societies

Looking backward in history, one can ask to what extent the geophysical factors, the natural and the artificial borders of territorial units, separate identities of populations and *Kulturkreise*, as well as the distinction between 'inside' and 'outside' – all the traditional objects of the science of geography – were in their essence merely the conceptual derivatives, or the material sediments/artifices of 'speed limits' – or, more generally, of the time-and-cost constraints imposed on freedom of movement.

Paul Virilio suggested recently that, while Francis Fukuyama's declaration of the 'end of history' looks grossly premature, one can with growing confidence speak presently of the 'end of geography'.[4] The distances do not matter any more, while the idea of a geophysical border is increasingly difficult to sustain in the 'real world'. It suddenly seems clear that the divisions of continents and of the globe as a whole were the function of distances made once imposingly real thanks to the primitiveness of transport and the hardships of travel.

Indeed, far from being an objective, impersonal, physical 'given', 'distance' is a social product; its length varies depending on the speed with which it may be overcome (and, in a monetary economy, on the cost involved in the attainment of that speed). All other socially produced factors of constitution, separation and the maintenance of collective identities – like state borders or cultural barriers – seem in retrospect merely secondary effects of that speed.

This seems to be the reason, let us note, why the 'reality of borders' was as a rule, most of the time, a class-stratified phenomenon: in the past, as they are today, the elites of the wealthy and the powerful were always more cosmopolitically inclined than the rest of the population of the lands they inhabited; at all times they tended to create a culture of their own which made little of the same borders that held fast for lesser folk; they had more in common with the elites across the borders than with the rest of the population inside them. This seems also to be the reason why Bill Clinton, the spokesman of the most powerful elite of the present-day world, could recently declare that for the first time there is no difference between domestic and foreign politics. Indeed, little in the elite's life experience now implies a difference between 'here' and 'there', 'inside' and 'outside', 'close by' and 'far away'. With time of communication imploding and shrinking to the no-size of the instant, space and spatial markers cease to matter, at least to those whose actions can move with the speed of the electronic message.

The 'inside' vs. 'outside', 'here' vs. out there', 'near' vs. 'far away' opposition recorded the degree of taming, domestication and familiarity of various fragments (human as much as inhuman) of the surrounding world.

Near, close to hand, is primarily what is usual, familiar and known to the point of obviousness; someone or something seen, met, dealt or interacted with daily, intertwined with habitual routine and day-to-day activities. 'Near' is a space inside which one can feel *chez soi*, at home; a space in which one seldom, if at all, finds oneself at a loss, feels lost for words or uncertain how to act. 'Far away', on the other hand, is a space which one enters only occasionally or not at all, in which things happen which one cannot anticipate or comprehend, and would not know how to react to once they occurred: a space containing things one knows little about, from which one does not expect much and regarding which one does not feel obliged to care. To find oneself in a 'far-away' space is an unnerving experience; venturing 'far away' means being beyond one's ken, out of place and out of one's element, inviting trouble and fearing harm.

Due to all such features, the 'near–far' opposition has one more, crucial dimension: that between certainty and uncertainty, self-assurance and hesitation. Being 'far away' means being in trouble – and so it demands cleverness, cunning, slyness or courage, learning foreign rules one can do without elsewhere, and mastering them through risky trials and often costly errors. The idea of the 'near', on the other hand, stands for the unproblematic; painlessly acquired habits will do, and since they are habits they feel weightless and call for no effort, giving no occasion to anxiety-prone hesitation. Whatever has come to be known as the 'local community' is brought into being by this opposition between 'here' and 'out there', 'near' and 'far away'.

Modern history has been marked by the constant progress of the means of transportation. Transport and travel was the field of particularly radical and rapid change; progress here, as Schumpeter pointed out a long time ago, was not the result of multiplying the number of stage-coaches, but of the invention and mass production of totally new means of travel – trains, motorcars and airplanes. It was primarily the availability of means of fast travel that triggered the typically modern process of eroding and undermining all locally entrenched social and cultural 'totalities'; the process first captured by Tönnies' famous formula of modernity as the passage from *Gemeinschaft* to *Gesellschaft*.

Among all the technical factors of mobility, a particularly great role was played by the transport of information – the kind of communication which does not involve movement of physical bodies or involves it only secondarily and marginally. Technical means were steadily and consistently developed which also allowed information to travel independently from its bodily carriers – and also from the objects of which the information informed: means which set the 'signifiers' free from the hold of the 'signifieds'. The separation of the movements of information from those of its carriers and its objects allowed in its turn the differentiation of their speed; the movement of information gathered speed on a pace much faster than the travel of bodies, or the change of the situations of which the information informed, was able to reach. In the end, the appearance of the computer-served World Wide Web put paid – as far as information is concerned – to the very notion of 'travel' (and of 'distance' to be travelled) and renders information, in theory as well as in practice, instantaneously available throughout the globe.

The overall results of the latest development are enormous. Its impact on the interplay of social association/dissociation has been widely noted and described in great detail. Much as one notices the 'essence of hammer' only when the hammer has been broken, we now see more clearly than ever before the role played by time, space and the means of saddling them in the formation, stability/flexibility, and the demise of socio/cultural and political totalities. The so-called 'closely knit communities' of yore were, as we can now see, brought into being and kept alive by the gap between the nearly instantaneous communication *inside* the small-scale community (the size of which was determined by the innate qualities of 'wetware', and thus confined to the natural limits of human sight, hearing and memorizing capacity) and the enormity of time and expense needed to pass information *between* localities. On the other hand, the present-day fragility and short life-span of communities appears primarily to be the result of that gap shrinking or altogether disappearing: inner-community communication has no advantage over inter-communal exchange, if *both* are instantaneous.

Michael Benedikt thus summarizes our retrospective discovery and the new understanding of the intimate connection between the speed of travel and social cohesion:

> The kind of unity made possible in small communities by the near-simultaneity and near-zero cost of natural voice communications, posters and leaflets, collapses at the larger scale. Social cohesion at any scale is a function of consensus, of shared knowledge, and without constant updating and interaction, such

cohesion depends crucially on early, and strict, education in –
and memory of – culture. Social flexibility, conversely, depends
on forgetting and cheap communication.[5]

Let us add that the 'and' in the last quoted sentence is
superfluous; the facility to forget, and cheapness (as well as the
high velocity) of communication, are but two aspects of the
same condition and could hardly be thought of separately.
Cheap communication means quick overflowing, stifling or
elbowing away the information acquired as much as it means
the speedy arrival of news. The capacities of 'wetware' remaining largely unchanged since at least palaeolithic times, cheap
communication floods and smothers memory rather than feeding and stabilizing it. Arguably the most seminal of recent
developments is the dwindling differences between the costs of
transmitting information on a local and global scale (wherever
you send your message through the Internet, you pay by the
tariff of the 'local call', a circumstance as important culturally
as it is economically); this, in turn, means that the information
eventually arriving and clamouring for attention, for entry to,
and (however short-lived) staying in the memory, tends to be
originated in the most diverse and mutually autonomous sites
and thus likely to convey mutually incompatible or mutually
cancelling messages – in sharp contradiction to the messages
floating inside communities devoid of hardware and software
and relying on 'wetware' only; that is, to the messages which
tended to reiterate and reinforce each other and assist the
process of (selective) memorizing.

As Timothy W. Luke puts it, 'the spatiality of traditional
societies is organized around the mostly unmediated capacities
of ordinary human bodies':

> Traditional visions of action often resort to organic metaphors
> for their allusions: conflict was chin-to-chin. Combat was hand-
> to-hand. Justice was an eye-for-an-eye, a-tooth-for-a-tooth.

Debate was heart-to-heart. Solidarity was shoulder-to-shoulder. Community was face-to-face. Friendship was arm-in-arm. And, change was step-by-step.

This situation had changed beyond recognition with the advance of means which allowed the stretching of conflicts, solidarities, combats, debates or the administration of justice well beyond the reach of the human eye and arm. Space had become 'processed/centred/organized/normalized', and above all emancipated from the natural constraint of the human body. It was therefore the capacity of technics, the speed of its action and the cost of its use which from then on 'organized space': 'The space projected by such technics is radically different: engineered, not God-given; artificial, not natural; mediated by hardware, not immediate to wetware; rationalized, not communalized; national, not local.'[6]

Engineered, modern space was to be tough, solid, permanent and non-negotiable. Concrete and steel were to be its flesh, the web of railway tracks and highways its blood vessels. Writers of modern utopias did not distinguish between social and architectural order, social and territorial units and divisions; for them – as for their contemporaries in charge of social order – the key to an orderly society was to be found in the organization of space. Social totality was to be a hierarchy of ever larger and more inclusive localities, with the supra-local authority of the state perched on the top and surveilling the whole, while itself protected from day-to-day invigilation.

Over that territorial/urbanistic/architectural, engineered space a third, *cybernating* space of the human world has been imposed with the advent of the global web of information. Elements of this space, according to Paul Virilio, are 'devoid of spatial dimensions, but inscribed in the singular temporality of an instantaneous diffusion. From here on, people can't be separated by physical obstacles or by temporal distances. With the interfacing of computer terminals and video-monitors, distinctions of *here* and *there* no longer mean anything.'[7]

Like most statements pronouncing on the 'human' condition as such – one and the same for all humans – this one is not exactly correct. The 'interfacing of computer terminals' has had a varied impact on the plight of different kinds of people. And some people – in fact, quite a lot of them – still can, as before, be 'separated by physical obstacles and temporal distances', this separation being now more merciless, and having more profound psychological effects, than ever before.

New speed, new polarization

To put it in a nutshell: *rather than homogenizing the human condition, the technological annulment of temporal/spatial distances tends to polarize it.* It emancipates certain humans from territorial constraints and renders certain community-generating meanings exterritorial – while denuding the territory, to which other people go on being confined, of its meaning and its identity-endowing capacity. For some people it augurs an unprecedented freedom from physical obstacles and unheard-of ability to move and act from a distance. For others, it portends the impossibility of appropriating and domesticating the locality from which they have little chance of cutting themselves free in order to move elsewhere. With 'distances no longer meaning anything', localities, separated by distances, also lose their meanings. This, however, augurs freedom of meaning-creation for some, but portends ascription to meaning-lessness for others. Some can now move out of the locality – any locality – at will. Others watch helplessly the sole locality they inhabit moving away from under their feet.

Information now floats independently from its carriers; shifting of bodies and rearrangement of bodies in physical space is less than ever necessary to reorder meanings and relationships.

For some people – for the mobile elite, the elite of mobility – this means, literally, the 'dephysicalization', the new weightlessness of power. Elites travel in space, and travel faster than ever before – but the spread and density of the power web they weave is not dependent on that travel. Thanks to new 'bodylessness' of power in its mainly financial form, the power-holders become truly exterritorial even if, bodily, they happen to stay 'in place'. Their power is, fully and truly, not 'out of this world' – not of the physical world in which they build their heavily guarded homes and offices, themselves exterritorial, free from intrusion of unwelcome neighbours, cut out from whatever may be called a *local* community, inaccessible to whoever is, unlike them, confined to it.

It is this new elite's experience of non-terrestriality of power – of the eerie yet awesome combination of ethereality with omnipotence, non-physicality and reality-forming might – which is being recorded in the common eulogy of the 'new freedom' embodied in electronically sustained 'cyberspace'; most remarkably, in Margaret Wertheim's 'analogy between cyberspace and the Christian conception of heaven':

> Just as early Christians envisaged heaven as an idealized realm beyond the chaos and decay of the material world – a disintegration all too palpable as the empire crumbled around them – so too, in this time of social and environmental disintegration, today's proselytizers of cyberspace proffer their domain as an ideal 'above' and 'beyond' the problems of the material world. While early Christians promulgated heaven as a realm in which the human soul would be freed from the frailties and failings of the flesh, so today's champions of cyberspace hail it as a place where the self will be freed from the limitations of physical embodiment.[8]

In cyberspace, bodies do not matter – though cyberspace matters, and matters decisively and irrevocably, in the life of bodies. There is no appeal from the verdicts passed in the cyberspatial heaven, and nothing that happens on earth may question their authority. With the power to pass verdicts securely vested in cyberspace, the bodies of the powerful need not be powerful bodies nor need they be armed with heavy material weapons; more than that, unlike Antheus, they need no link to their earthly environment to assert, ground or manifest their power. What they need is the isolation from locality, now stripped of social meaning which has been transplanted into cyberspace, and so reduced to a merely 'physical' terrain. What they also need is *the security of that isolation* – a 'non-neighbourhood' condition, immunity from local interference, a foolproof, invulnerable isolation, translated as the 'safety' of persons, of their homes and their playgrounds. Deterritorialization of power therefore goes hand in hand with the ever stricter structuration of the territory.

In a study with the telling-it-all title 'Building Paranoia', Steven Flusty notes the breathtaking explosion of ingenuity and a most frenetic building boom in a field new to the metropolitan areas: that of the 'interdictory spaces' – 'designed to intercept and repel or filter would-be users'. Flusty deploys his unique knack for coining precisely targeted and poignantly suggestive terms to distinguish several varieties of such spaces which supplement each other and combine into a new urban equivalent of the moats and turrets that once guarded medieval castles. Among such varieties, there is 'slippery space' – 'space that cannot be reached, due to contorted, protracted, or missing paths of approach'; 'prickly space' – 'space that cannot be comfortably occupied, defended by such details as wall-mounted sprinkler heads activated to clear loiterers or ledges sloped to inhibit sitting'; or 'jittery space' – 'space that cannot be utilized unobserved due to active monitoring by roving patrols and/or remote technologies feeding to security stations'. These and other 'interdictory spaces' serve no other purpose than to re-forge the social exterritoriality of the new supra-local elite into the material, bodily isolation from locality. They also put a final touch on the disintegration of locally grounded forms of togetherness and shared, communal living. The exterritoriality of elites is assured in the most material fashion – their physical inaccessibility to anyone not issued with an entry permit.

In a complementary development, such urban spaces where the occupants of different residential areas could meet face-to-face, engage in casual encounters, accost and challenge one another, talk, quarrel, argue or agree, lifting their private problems to the level of public issues and making public issues into matters of private concern – those 'private/public' agoras of Cornelius Castoriadis's – are fast shrinking in size and number. The few that remain tend to be increasingly selective – adding strengths to, rather than repairing the damage done by the push of disintegrating forces. As Steven Flusty puts it,

> traditional public spaces are increasingly supplanted by privately produced (though often publicly subsidized), privately owned and administered spaces for public aggregation, that is, spaces of consumption . . . [A]ccess is predicated upon ability to pay . . . Exclusivity rules here, ensuring the high levels of control necessary to prevent irregularity, unpredictability, and inefficiency from interfering with the orderly flow of commerce.[9]

The elites have *chosen* isolation and pay for it lavishly and *willingly*. The rest of the population *finds itself* cut off and *forced* to pay the heavy cultural, psychological and political price of their new isolation. Those unable to make their separate living the matter of choice and to pay the costs of its security are on the receiving side of the contemporary equivalent of the early-modern enclosures; they are purely and simply 'fenced off' without having been asked their consent, barred access to yesterday's 'commons', arrested, turned back and facing a short sharp shock when blundering into the off-limits regions, failing to note the 'private property' warning signs or to read the meaning of the non-verbalized, yet no less resolute for that reason, the 'no trespassing' hints and clues.

Urban territory becomes the battlefield of continuous space war, sometimes erupting into the public spectacle of inner-city riots, ritual skirmishes with the police, the occasional forays of soccer crowds, but waged daily just beneath the surface of the public (publicized), official version of the routine urban order. Disempowered and disregarded residents of the 'fenced-off', pressed-back and relentlessly encroached-upon areas, respond with aggressive action of their own; they try to install on the borders of their ghettoized home ground 'no trespassing' signs of their own making. Following the eternal custom of *bricoleurs* they use for the purpose any material they can lay their hands on – 'rituals, dressing strangely, striking bizarre attitudes, breaking rules, breaking bottles, windows, heads, issuing rhetorically challenges to the law'.[10] Effective or not, these attempts have the handicap of non-authorization and tend to be conveniently classified, in the official records, as issues of law and order, rather than what they are in fact: attempts to make their territorial claims audible and legible and so merely to follow the new rules of the territoriality game everyone else is playing with gusto.

The fortifications built by the elite and the self-defence-through-aggression practised by those left outside the walls have a mutually reinforcing effect clearly predicted by Gregory Bateson's theory of 'schismogenetic chains'. According to that theoretical model, schism is likely to emerge and deepen beyond repair when a position is set up in which

> the behaviour X, Y, Z is the standard reply to X, Y, Z . . . If, for example, the patterns X, Y, Z include boasting, we shall see that there is a likelihood, if boasting is the reply to boasting, that each group will drive the other into excessive emphasis of the pattern, a process which if not restrained can only lead to more and more

extreme rivalry and ultimately to hostility and the breakdown of the whole system.

The above is the pattern of 'symmetrical differentiation'. What is its alternative? What happens if group B fails to respond to the X, Y, Z kind of challenge by group A with an X, Y, Z type of behaviour? The schismogenetic chain is not then cut – it only assumes the pattern of 'complementary', instead of symmetrical, differentiation. If, for instance, assertive behaviour is not responded to in the same currency, but meets with submissiveness, 'it is likely that this submissiveness will promote further assertiveness which in turn will promote further submissiveness'. The 'breakdown of the system' will follow all the same.[11]

The overall effect of the choice between the two patterns is minimal, but for the sides tied by the schismogenetic chain the difference between the patterns is one between dignity and humiliation, humanity and its loss. One can safely anticipate that the strategy of symmetrical differentiation would be always preferred to the complementary alternative. The latter is the strategy for the defeated or for those who accepted inevitability of defeat. Some things, though, are bound to emerge victorious, whatever strategy is chosen: the new fragmentation of the city space, the shrinkage and disappearance of public space, the falling apart of urban community, separation and segregation – and above all the exterritoriality of the new elite and the forced territoriality of the rest.

If the new exterritoriality of the elite feels like intoxicating freedom, the territoriality of the rest feels less like home ground, and ever more like prison – all the more humiliating for the obtrusive sight of the others' freedom to move. It is not just that the condition of 'staying put', being unable to move at one's heart's desire and being barred access to greener pastures, exudes the acrid odour of defeat, signals incomplete humanity and implies being cheated in the division of splendours life has to offer. Deprivation reaches deeper. The 'locality' in the new world of high speed is not what the locality used to be at a time when information moved only together with the bodies of its carriers; neither the locality, nor the localized population has much in common with the 'local community'. Public spaces – agoras and forums in their various manifestations, places where agendas are set, private affairs are made public, opinions are formed, tested and confirmed, judgements are put together and verdicts are passed – such spaces followed the elite in cutting lose their local anchors; they are first to deterritorialize and move far beyond the reach of the merely 'wetware' communicative capacity of any locality and its residents. Far from being hotbeds of communities, local populations are more like loose bunches of untied ends.

Paul Lazarsfeld wrote of the 'local opinion leaders', who sift, evaluate and process for other locals the messages which arrive from the 'outside' through the media; but to do so, the local leaders must first have been heard by the locality – they needed an agora where the locals could come together to talk and listen. It was that local agora which allowed the voice of the local opinion leaders' to compete with the voices from afar and gain conviction able to outweigh the much more resourceful authority, thinned as it was by its distance. I doubt whether Lazarsfeld would come to the same conclusion were he to repeat his study today, a mere half-century later.

Nils Christie has recently tried to encapsulate, in an allegory, the logic of the process and its consequences.[12] Since the text is not yet easily available, I will quote the story at length:

> Moses came down from the mountains. Under his arm he carried the rules, engraved in granite, dictated to him by one even further up than the mountains. Moses was only a messenger, the people – the populus – were the receivers ... Much later, Jesus and Mohammed functioned according to the same principles. These are classical cases of '*pyramidal justice*'.
>
> And then the other picture: females gathering at the water-

fountain, the well, or at natural meeting places along the river
. . . Fetch water, wash the clothes, and exchange informations
and evaluations. The point of departure for their conversation
will often be the concrete acts and situations. These are *described*,
compared to similar occurences in the past and somewhere else,
and *evaluated* – right or wrong, beautiful or ugly, strong or weak.
Slowly, but far from always, some common understanding of the
occurrences might emerge. This is a process whereby norms are
created. It is a classical case of *'equalitarian justice'* . . .

. . .[T]he water well is abolished. We had in modernized
countries for a while some small shops with coin-operated
Laundromats where we could come with our dirty linen and
leave with the clean ones. In the intervals, there was some time
to talk. Now the Laundromats are gone . . . Huge shopping malls
might give some opportunities for encounters, but mostly they
are too large for the creation of horizontal justice. Too large to
find the old acquaintances and too busy and crowded for the
prolonged chats needed to establish standards for behaviour . . .

Let me add that the shopping malls are so constructed as to
keep people moving, looking around, keep them diverted and
entertained no end – but in no case for too long – by any of the
endless attractions; not to encourage them to stop, look at each
other, talk to each other, think of, ponder and debate something
other than the objects on display – not to pass their time in a
fashion devoid of commercial value . . .

Christie's allegorical account has the extra merit of bringing
to the surface the ethical effects of the demotion of public
spaces. The meeting places were also the sites in which *norms
were created* – so that justice could be done, and apportioned
horizontally, thus re-forging the conversationalists into a *community*, set apart and integrated by the shared criteria of
evaluation. Hence a territory stripped of public space provides
little chance for norms being debated, for values to be confronted, to clash and to be negotiated. The verdicts of right and
wrong, beauty and ugliness, proper and improper, useful and

useless may only descend from on high, from regions never to be penetrated by any but a most inquisitive eye; the verdicts are unquestionable since no questions may be meaningfully addressed to the judges and since the judges left no address – not even an e-mail address – and no one can be sure where they reside. No room is left for the 'local opinion leaders'; no room is left for the 'local opinion' as such.

The verdicts may be completely out of touch with the way life runs locally, but they are not meant to be tested in the experience of people on whose conduct they pronounce. Born out of a kind of experience known to the local receivers of the message through hearsay at best, they may rebound in more suffering even if they intend to bring joy. The exterritorial originals enter locally-bound life only as caricatures; perhaps as mutants and monsters. On the way, they expropriate the ethical powers of the locals, depriving them of all means of limiting the damage.

2

Space Wars: a Career Report

It is often said, and yet more often taken for granted, that the idea of 'social space' was born (in sociologists' heads, of course – where else?) of a metaphorical transposition of concepts formed within the experience of physical, 'objective' space. The opposite is the case, though. That distance, which we are now inclined to call 'objective' and to measure by comparing it with the length of the equator, rather than with the size of human bodily parts, corporal dexterity or sympathies/antipathies of its inhabitants, used to be measured by human bodies and human relations long before the metal rod called the metre, that impersonality and disembodiment incarnate, was deposited at Sèvres for everyone to respect and obey.

The great social historian Witold Kula demonstrated more thoroughly than any other scholar that not only in the subtle sense derived from the philosophical ruminations of Protagoras, but in a quite mundane, literal sense, and in an utterly unphilosophical mode, the human body was, since time immemorial, 'the measure of everything'. Throughout their history and until the quite recent advent of modernity humans measured the world with their bodies – feet, handfuls or elbows; with their products – baskets or pots; with their activities – dividing, for instance, their fields into 'Morgen', that is into plots which could be ploughed up by a man working from dawn to dusk.

One handful is not, though, like another, nor is one basket as big as another; the 'anthropomorphic' and 'praxeomorphic' measures were bound to be as diversified and contingent as the human bodies and human practices to which they referred. Hence the difficulty, arising whenever the power-holders wished to accord a uniform treatment to a larger number of subjects, demanding from them all 'the same' taxes or levies. A way had then to be found to bypass and neutralize the impact of variety and contingency – and it was found in the imposition of standard, and binding, measures of distance, surface or volume, while forbidding all other local, group- or individual-based, renditions.

Not just the question of measuring the space 'objectively' presented a problem, however. Before it may come to measuring, one needs first to have a clear notion of what is there to be measured. If it is space that is to be measured (or indeed conceived of as something measurable), one needs first the idea of 'distance' – and that idea was in its origins parasitic on the distinction between things or people 'close' and 'far away', and the experience of some things or people being 'closer' to one than some others. Drawing inspiration from Durkheim/Mauss's thesis of the social origins of classification, Edmund Leach documented the astonishing parallelity between the popular categorizations of space, kinship classification and the differentiated treatment of domestic, farm and wild animals.[1] The categories of home, farm, field and the 'far away' appear to be set apart in the popular map of the world on a very similar, virtually the same, principle, as the categories of domestic pets, farm cattle, game and 'wild animals' on the one hand, and the categories of sister/brother, cousin, neighbour and the alien or 'foreigner' on the other.

As Claude Lévi-Strauss suggested, the prohibition of incest, which implied the imposition of artificial, conceptual distinctions upon individuals physically, bodily, 'naturally' undifferentiated, was the first – constitutive – act of culture, which was to consist forever hence in the insertion into the 'natural' world of the divisions, distinctions and classifications which reflected the differentiation of human practice and practice-bound concepts, and were not the attributes of 'nature' on its own but of human activity and thought. The task confronted by the modern state faced with the necessity of the unification of space subjected now to its direct rule was no exception; it consisted in disentangling the spatial categories and distinctions from such human practices which the state powers did not control. The task boiled down to the substitution of administrative practices of the state for all other, local and disperse practices, as the sole and universally binding reference point for all measures and divisions of space.

The battle of the maps

What is easily legible or transparent for some, can be dark and opaque for others. Where some make their way without the slightest difficulty, others may feel disoriented and lost. As long as the measures remained anthropomorphic and had varied and mutually uncoordinated local practices for their reference points, they served human communities as a shield behind which they could hide from curious eyes and hostile intentions of intruders, above all from the impositions of intruders with superior powers.

In order to collect taxes and recruit soldiers, pre-modern powers, incapable of reading out the realities fully legible to their subjects, had to behave like alien, hostile forces: to resort to armed invasions and punitive expeditions. Indeed, there was little to distinguish the practice of tax-collection from robbery and looting, and the practice of enlisting soldiers from that of taking prisoners; the armed hirelings of barons and princes persuaded 'the natives' to part with their produce or their sons using swords and whips as arguments; they managed to get as much as the display of brutal force allowed them to squeeze. Ernest Gellner dubbed the pre-modern system of rule as the 'dentistry state': the rulers specialized, he wrote, in extraction through torture.

Baffled and confused by the bewildering variety of local measures and counting systems, taxing powers and their agents preferred as a rule to deal with corporations rather than individual subjects, with village or parish elders rather than with individual farmers or tenants; even in the case of taxes as 'individualized' and 'personal' as the levies charged on chimneys or windows, state authorities preferred to allocate a global quota to the village, leaving the distribution of burdens to the locals. One can also suppose that a decisive reason to prefer the payment of taxes in currency to taxes paid in agricultural produce was the independence of currency values, determined by the state-run mint, from local custom. In the absence of the 'objective' measurements of land holdings, of land registers and inventory of cattle, indirect taxes – levied on activities difficult or impossible to hide in the thicket of interactions obvious to the locals but impenetrable and misleading to occasional visitors (for instance, taxes charged on the sale of salt or tobacco, road and bridge tolls, payments for offices and titles) – were the means of obtaining income favoured by the pre-modern state, which, as Charles Lindblom aptly put it, had thumbs only but no fingers.

No wonder that the legibility of space, its transparency, has turned into one of the major stakes in the modern state's battle for sovereignty of its powers. In order to gain legislative, regulatory control over the patterns of social interaction and loyalties – the state had to gain control over the transparency of the setting, in which various agents involved in the interaction are obliged to act. The modernization of social arrangements, promoted by the practices of modern powers, aimed at the establishment and perpetuation of control so understood. One decisive aspect of the modernizing process was therefore the protracted war waged in the name of the reorganization of space. The stake of the major battle in that war was the right to control the cartographic office.

The elusive goal of the modern space war was the subordination of social space to one and only one, officially approved and state-sponsored map – an effort coupled with and supported by the disqualification of all other, competitive maps or interpretations of space, as well as the dismantling or disabling of all cartographic institutions and endeavours other than the state-established, state-endowed or state-licensed. The space structure to emerge at the end of that space war was to be one perfectly legible for the state power and its agents, while remaining thoroughly immune to semantic processing by its users or victims – resistant to all 'grass-roots' interpretative initiatives which could yet saturate fragments of space with meanings unknown and illegible to the powers-that-be, and so make such fragments invulnerable to control from above.

The invention of painterly perspective, accomplished in the fifteenth century by the joint efforts of Alberti and Brunelleschi, was a decisive step and a genuine turning point on the long road to the modern conception of space and the modern methods of its implementation. The idea of perspective lay mid-way between the vision of space firmly embedded in collective and individual realities and its later modern disembeddedment. It took for granted the decisive role of human perception in the organization of space: the viewer's eye was the starting point of all perspective; it determined the size and mutual distances of all objects falling into this field and remained the sole reference point for the allocation of objects and space. The novelty, though, was that the viewer's eye was now a 'human eye as such', a brand new, 'impersonal' eye. It did not matter now who were the viewers; the only circumstance which counted was that they placed themselves at the given point of observation. It has now been asserted –

indeed, taken for granted – that *any viewer* placed in that point will see the spatial relations between objects in exactly the same way.

From now on, not the qualities of the viewer, but the fully quantifiable location of the observation point, the location plottable in an abstract and empty, human-free space, socially/ culturally indifferent and impersonal space, was to decide the spatial arrangement of things. The conception of perspective achieved a double feat, thereby harnessing the praxeomorphic nature of distance to the needs of the new homogeneity promoted by the modern state. While acknowledging the subjective relativity of space maps, it simultaneously neutralized the impact of that relativity: it depersonalized the consequences of the subjective origins of perceptions almost as radically as Husserl's image of meaning born of 'transcendental' subjectivity.

The point of gravity in spatial organization has been shifted thereby from the question 'Who?' to the question 'From what point in space?' Once that question had been posited, though, it immediately became evident that, since not every human creature occupies the same place and thus contemplates the world from the same perspective, not all sightings are likely to be equal in value. There must be or should be, therefore, a certain privileged point from which the best perception can be attained. It was now easy to see that the 'best' meant 'objective', which in its turn meant non- or supra-personal. The 'best' was such a unique reference point as would be capable of accomplishing the miracle, of rising above, and overcoming, its own endemic relativity.

The pre-modern chaotic and bewildering diversity of maps was to be replaced therefore not so much with one universally shared image of the world, as with a strict hierarchy of images. Theoretically, the 'objective' meant first and foremost 'superior', while its practical superiority remained the ideal state of affairs yet for the modern powers to attain – and once achieved, it would become one of those powers' principal resources.

Territories fully domesticated, thoroughly familiar and intelligible for the purposes of the day-to-day activities of the villagers or parishioners remained confusingly and threateningly alien, inaccessible and untamed to the authorities in the capital; the reversal of that relationship was one of the main dimensions and indices of the 'modernization process'.

The legibility and transparency of space, declared in modern times to be the distinctive mark of rational order, were not, as such, modern inventions; after all, in all times and places they were indispensable conditions of human cohabitation, offering the modicum of certainty and self-assurance without which daily life was all but unthinkable. The sole modern novelty was the positing of transparency and legibility as a goal to be systematically pursued – a *task*; something which still needs to be enforced on recalcitrant reality, having first been carefully designed with the help of specialists' expertise. Modernization meant, among other things, making the populated world hospitable for supra-communal, state-ruled administration; and that task required, as its necessary condition, making the world transparent and legible for administrative powers.

In his seminal study of the 'bureaucratic phenomenon' Michel Crozier has shown the intimate connection between the certainty/uncertainty scale and the hierarchy of power. We learn from Crozier that in any structured (organized) collectivity the ruling position belongs to such units as make their own situation opaque and their actions impenetrable for the outsiders – while keeping them clear to themselves – free from misty spots and secure against surprises. Throughout the world of modern bureaucracies the strategy of every extant or aspiring sector consists invariably and consistently in attempts to untie its own hands, and the pressure to impose strict and stringent rules on the conduct of everyone else within the organization. Such a sector gains most influence, as manages to make its own behaviour an unknown variable in the equations which other sectors compose in order to make their choices – while succeeding in rendering the other sectors' conduct constant, regular and predictable. In other words, most power is exercised by such units as manage to remain the sources of other units' uncertainty. The manipulation of uncertainty is the essence and the primary stake in the struggle for power and influence inside every structured totality – first and foremost in its most radical form, that of the modern bureaucratic organization, and particularly the modern state bureaucracy.

Michel Foucault's panoptical model of modern power rests on a very similar assumption. The decisive factor in that power which the supervisors hidden in the Panopticon's central tower wield over the inmates held in the wings of the star-like building, is the combination of full and constant visibility of the latter with the equally complete and perpetual invisibility of the former. Never sure whether the supervisors are watching them, whether their attention is diverted to other wings, whether they are asleep, resting or otherwise engaged, the inmates must at all times behave *as if* they were currently under surveillance. The supervisors and the inmates (be they prisoners, workers, soldiers, pupils, patients or whatever) reside inside 'the same' space, but are cast in diametrically opposite situations. The vision of the first group is unobstructed, while the second needs to act in a misty and opaque territory.

Let us note that Panopticon was an *artificial space* – built on purpose, with the asymmetry of seeing ability in mind. The purpose was to manipulate consciously and rearrange wilfully the transparency of space as social relation – as, in the last account, a power relationship. The artificiality of made-to-order space was a luxury not available to the powers bent on manipulating space on a state-wide scale. Instead of creating a new, functionally impeccable space from scratch, modern state powers – while pursuing 'panoptical' objectives – had to settle for the second-best solution. Mapping the space in a way easily legible for the state administration, yet going against the grain of local practices, depriving the 'locals' of their well mastered means of orientation and therefore confusing, was thus the first strategic task of the modern space war. The panoptical ideal was not, however, abandoned; it was merely put on a back burner, waiting for more potent technology. The first stage having achieved its ends, the road could be open for the next, yet more ambitious stage of the modernizing process. In that stage, the goal was not just the *charting* of elegant, uniform and uniformizing maps of state territory, but *reshaping the space* physically after the pattern of the elegance thus far achieved only by the charts drafted and stored inside the cartographic office; not to settle for perfectly recording the territory's extant imperfection, but encrusting on the land the degree of perfection previously seen only on the drawing board.

Before, it was the map which reflected and recorded the shapes of the territory. Now, it was the turn of the territory to become a reflection of the map, to be raised to the level of orderly transparency which the maps struggled to reach. It was the space itself which was to be reshaped or shaped up from scratch in the likeness of the map and according to the decisions of cartographers.

From mapping space to the spatialization of maps

Intuitively, it is the geometrically simple space structure, put together of uniform blocks of the same size, which seems to come nearest to meeting the above demand. No wonder that, in all modern utopian visions of the 'perfect city', the urbanistic and architectural rules which the authors treated with untired and unrelenting attention circled around the same basic principles: first, the strict, detailed and comprehensive, advance *planning* of the city space – construction of the city 'from scratch', on an empty or emptied site, according to a design completed before the construction began; and second, the regularity, uniformity, homogeneity, reproductibility of the space elements surrounding the administrative buildings placed in the centre of the city, or better still on the top of a hill from which the whole of the city space can be visually embraced. The following 'fundamental and sacred laws' composed by Morelly in his *Code de la Nature, ou le véritable esprit de ses lois de tout temps négligé ou méconnu*, published in 1755, offer a representative example of modern concept of the perfectly structured space of the city.

> Around a large square of *regular proportions* [here and below italics added – Z.B.] public warehouses will be erected storing all the necessary supplies and entailing the hall for public gatherings – everything of the uniform and pleasant appearance.
> On the outside of that circle city districts will be *regularly* arranged – each of *the same* size, *similar* form, and divided by *equal* streets . . .
> All buildings will be *identical* . . .
> All districts will be so planned, tht if needs be they may be expanded *without disturbing their regularity* . . .

The principles of uniformity and regularity (and thus also of exchangeability) of city elements were complemented, in the thought of Morelly as well as of the other visionaries and practitioners of the modern city planning and administration, by the postulate of the functional subordination of all the architectural and demographic solutions to the 'needs of the city as a whole' (as Morelly himself put it, 'the number and size' of all buildings will be dictated by the needs of a given town'), and the demand to separate spatially parts of the city dedicated to different functions or differing in the quality of their inhabitants. And so 'each tribe will occupy a separate district, and each family a separate apartment'. (The buildings, however, Morelly hastens to emphasize, will be the same for all families; this requirement could have been dictated, one may guess, by the wish to neutralize the potentially detrimental impact of idiosyncratic tribal traditions on the overall transparency of the city space.) Such residents as for whatever reason failed to meet the standards of normality ('ill citizens', 'invalid and senile citizens', and such as 'will deserve a temporary isolation from the rest') will be confined to the areas 'outside all circles, at a certain distance'. Finally, residents deserving '*civic* death, that is life-long exclusion from society', will be locked in cave-like cells of 'very strong walls and bars', next to the *biologically* dead, inside the 'walled-off graveyard'.

The likenesses of the perfect city, drafted by the utopists' pens, did not resemble any real cities, in which the draughtsmen lived and dreamed. But, as Karl Marx was to point out a little later (with a nod of approval), their concern was not with how to represent or explain the world, but how to change it. Or, rather, they resented the constraints which extant reality imposed on the implementation of ideal designs, and dreamed of replacing it with a new reality, free of the morbid traces of historical accidents, made from scratch and to order. The 'small print' of every project of a city yet to be created *ab nihilo* implied the destruction of a city already in existence. In the midst of the present – messy, fetid, rambling and chaotic, and thus deserving a death sentence – utopian thought was a bridgehead of future orderly perfection and perfect order.

Fantasy, however, is seldom genuinely 'idle' and even less frequently is it truly innocent. Not just in the heated imagination of the draughtsmen were their blueprints footholds of the future. There was no shortage of armies and the generals eager to use the utopian bridgeheads to launch an all-out assault against the powers of chaos and to help the future to invade and conquer the present. In his eye-opening study of modern utopias Bronisław Baczko speaks of 'a double movement: that of the utopian imagination to conquer urban space and that of dreams of city planning and of architecture in search of a social framework in which they can materialize'.[2] The thinkers and the doers of things were in equal measure obsessed with 'the centre', around which the space of the future cities was to be logically arranged, thereby meeting the conditions of transparency set by impersonal reason. That obsession in all its interconnected aspects is masterly dissected in Baczko's analysis of the project of the 'City named Liberty', published on 12 Floréal of the year V of the French Republic by the surveyor-geometrician F.-L. Aubry – and meant as the blueprint sketch for the future capital of revolutionary France.

For theorists and practitioners alike the future city was a spatial incarnation, symbol and monument of freedom, won by Reason in its protracted life-and-death war against unruly, irrational contingency of history; just as the freedom promised by the revolution was to purify historical time, the space dreamed up by the urban utopians was to be a site 'never polluted by history'. This stern condition eliminated from the competition all extant cities, condemning them all to destruction.

True, Baczko focuses on only one among the numerous meeting places for dreamers and men of action – the French Revolution; but this was a place frequently visited by inspiration-seeking travellers from far and wide, as the encounter was there more than anywhere else intimate and joyfully celebrated by both partners. The dreams of the perfectly transparent city space served the political leaders of the revolution as a rich source of inspiration and courage, while for the dreamers the revolution was to be first and foremost a bold, determined and resourceful design-and-build company, ready to engrave on the building sites of perfect cities the forms conjured up during the endless sleepless nights spent over the utopian drawing boards.

Here is one of the many cases explored by Baczko: the story of the ideal land Sévarambes and its yet more perfect capital, Sévariade:[3]

> Sévariade is 'the most beautiful city in the world'; it is marked by 'the good maintenance of law and order'. 'The capital is con-

ceived according to a rational, clear, and simple plan, which is rigorously followed, and which makes this the most regular city in the world.' The transparency of city space drives mostly from the decision to divide neatly into 260 identical units – *osmasies*, each one being a square building with a façade 50 feet long, large court inside, four doors and one thousand inhabitants 'comfortably accommodated'. The city strikes the visitor with 'perfect regularity'. 'The streets are wide and so straight that one has the impression that they were laid out with a ruler' and all open on 'spacious plazas in the middle of which are fountains and public buildings' also of a uniform size and shape. 'The architecture of the houses is nearly uniform', though an extra sumptuousness marks the residences of important people. 'There is nothing chaotic in these cities: everywhere a perfect and striking order reigns' (the ill, the mentally handicapped and the criminals have been evicted beyond the boundaries of the city). Everything here has its function, and so everything is beautiful – as beauty means obviousness of purpose and simplicity of form. Nearly all the elements of the city are interchangeable – and so are the cities themselves; whoever visited Sévariade, knows all other cities of Sévarambes.

We do not know, Baczko observes, whether the draughtsmen of the perfect cities studied each other's projects – but their readers cannot but feel that 'throughout the century all they do is continually reinvent the same city'. This impression is caused by the values common to all composers of utopias, and their shared concern with 'a certain ideal of happy rationality or, if you will, of rational happiness' – implying a life conducted in a perfectly ordered space cleansed of all randomness – free from everything haphazard, accidental and ambivalent.

The cities described in the utopian literature are all, in Baczko's apt expression, '*literary* cities'; not just in the obvious sense of being products of literary imagination, but in another, deeper sense: they could be *recounted* in writing every minute detail, since they contained nothing ineffable, illegible, defying clear representation. Much like Jürgen Habermas's conception of the objective legitimacy of assertions and norms, which can be only universal and thus demands 'the effacing of space and time',[4] so the vision of the perfect city implied a total rejection of history and razing to the ground of all its tangible remnants. As a matter of fact, that vision challenged the authority of both space and time through the elimination of the qualitative differentiation of space which is always a sediment of equally differentiated, and thus historical, time.

The postulate of such 'dematerialization' of space and time blended with the idea of 'rational happiness' turns into a resolute, unconditional commandment once human reality is contemplated from the windows of administrative offices. It is only when seen through those windows that the diversity of space fragments, and particularly the open-endedness and under-determination of their destination, its amenability to multiple interpretations, seem to deny the chance of rational action. From this administrative perspective it is difficult to imagine a model of rationality distinct from one's own and a model of happiness different from living in a world bearing the impression of that rationality. Situations which lend themselves to many distinct definitions, situations which may be decoded with alternative keys, appear to be not just obstacles to the transparency of one's own field of action, but a drawback signalling 'opacity as such'; not a sign of the multiplicity of coexistent orders, but a symptom of chaos; not just a hindrance in the implementation of one's own model of rational action, but a state of affairs incompatible with 'reason as such'.

From the point of view of spatial administration, modernization means monopolization of cartographic rights. Monopoly is, however, impossible to retain in a palimpsest-like city, built of the layers of successive accidents of history; a city that has emerged and is still emerging out of a selective assimilation of divergent traditions and equally selective absorption of cultural innovations, with both selections having been subject to changing rules, rarely explicit, seldom present in thought at the time of action and amenable to quasi-logical codification only with the benefit of hindsight. Monopoly is much easier to achieve if the map precedes the mapped territory: if the city is, from its creation and for the duration of its entire history, simply a projection of the map upon the space; if, instead of desperately trying to capture the disorderly variety of urban reality in the impersonal elegance of a cartographic grid, the map turns into a frame in which urban realities yet to arise are to be plotted, deriving their meaning and function solely from the site allocated to them within the grid. Only then could the meanings and functions be truly unambiguous; their *Eindeutigkeit* will be vouched for in advance by disempowerment or the eviction of alternative interpretive authorities.

Of such a condition, ideal for the cartographic monopoly, dreamt openly the most radically modernist architects and urbanists of our era – Le Corbusier most famously among them. As if to demonstrate the supra-partisan nature of spatial modernization and the absence of any link between its principles and political ideologies, Corbusier offered his services with equal zeal and absence of scruples to the Communist rulers of Russia and the *fascisantes* rulers of Vichy France. As if to document the endemic nebulousness of modernist ambitions, he fell out with both: the involuntary yet inexorable pragmatism of the rulers was bound to cut the wings of radical imagination.

In *La ville radieuse*,[5] published in 1933 and destined to become the gospel of urban modernism, Corbusier passed a sentence of death on extant cities – the rotting refuse of unruly, thoughtless, urbanistically ignorant and hapless history. He charged existing cities with non-functionality (some logically indispensable functions having no satisfying agents, while some other functions overlap and clash, causing confusion in the city dwellers), with insalubrity, and with offence to the aesthetic sense (brought about by the chaotic maze of streets and architectural styles). The shortcomings of existing cities were much too numerous for the rectification of each one of them separately to be worth the effort and the resources required. It would be much more reasonable to apply a wholesale treatment and to cure all afflictions in one fell swoop – by razing the inherited cities to the ground and vacating their sites for the building of new cities, planned in advance in every detail; or by abandoning the Parises of today to their own morbid fate and transporting their residents to new sites, correctly conceived from the beginning. *La ville radieuse* presents the principles meant to guide the construction of the future cities, while focusing on the examples of Paris (impenitent, in spite of Baron Haussmann's bravado), Buenos Aires and Rio de Janeiro; all three projects start from the zero point, attending solely to the rules of aesthetic harmony and the impersonal logic of functional division.

In all three imagined capitals, functions are given priority over space; logic and aesthetics alike demand functional non-ambiguity of any fragment of the city. In the space of the city, just as in human life, one needs to distinguish and keep apart the functions of work, home life, shopping, entertainment, cult, administration; each function needs a place of its own, while every place should serve one and only one function.

Architecture, according to Corbusier, is – like logic and beauty – a born enemy of all confusion, spontaneity, chaos, messiness; architecture is a science akin to geometry, the art of platonic sublimity, mathematical orderliness, harmony; its ideals are the continuous line, parallels, right angle; its strategic principles are standardization and prefabrication. For the Radiant City of the future the rule of architecture aware of its vocation would therefore mean *the death of the street* as we know it – that incoherent and contingent by-product of uncoordinated and desynchronized building history, the battleground of incompatible uses and the site of accident and ambiguity. The tracks of the Radiant City, just like its buildings, will be consigned to specific tasks; in their case, the sole task will be that of traffic, of transporting people and goods from one functionally distinguished site to another, and that sole function will be cleansed of all present disturbances caused by aimless strollers, idlers, loiterers or just accidental passers-by.

Corbusier dreamt of a city in which the rule of 'le Plan dictateur' (he wrote the word 'plan' always with a capital 'P') over the residents will be complete and unquestioned. The authority of the Plan, derived from and grounded in the objective truths of logic and aesthetics, bears no dissent or controversy; it accepts no arguments that refer to, or seek support in, anything other than logical or aesthetical rigours. The actions of the city planner are therefore by their nature immune to the commotion of electoral excitements and deaf to the complaints of their genuine or imaginary victims. The 'Plan' (being the product of impersonal reason, not a figment of individual, however brilliant or profound, imagination) is the sole – both necessary and sufficient – condition of human happiness, which cannot rest on anything but the perfect fit between scientifically definable human needs and the unambiguous, transparent and legible arrangement of the living space.

La ville radieuse remained an exercise on paper. But at least one architect-urbanist, Oscar Niemeyer, attempted to make Corbusier's word flesh when the chance occurred. The chance in question was a commission to conjure up from scratch, in a desert-like void unburdened by history, a new capital matching the vastness, grandeur, huge untapped resources and unbound ambitions of Brazil. That capital, Brasilia, was the paradise for the modernist architect: here, at long last, the opportunity had come to brush aside all constraint and limitations, material or sentimental alike, and let loose the architectural fantasy

On a previously uninhabited plateau of central Brazil one could shape the residents of the future city at will, concerned only with loyalty to logic and aesthetics; and do it without any need to compromise, let alone sacrifice the purity of principles to irrelevant yet obstinate circumstances of place and time. One could calculate precisely and well in advance the yet inarticulate and inchoate 'unit needs'; one could compose, unhampered, the yet-non-existing, and therefore silent and politically power-less, inhabitants of the future city, as aggregates of scientifically defined and carefully measured needs for oxygen, thermal and lighting units.

For experimenters more interested in a job well done than in its effects on those on the receiving end of their actions, Brasilia was a huge and lavishly subsidized laboratory, in which various ingredients of logic and aesthetics could be mixed together in varying proportions, their reactions observed in an unadulter-ated form, and the most pleasing compound selected. As the assumptions of the Corbusier-style architectural modernism suggested, one could in Brasilia design a space made to the measure of man (or, to be more exact, of all that in man which is measurable), and thus a space from which accident and surprise was evicted and barred return. For its residents, though, Brasilia proved to be nightmare. Quickly a concept of 'brasilitis', the new pathological syndrome of which Brasilia was the prototype and the most famous epicentre to date, was coined by its hapless victims. The most conspicuous symptoms of brasilitis, by common consent, were the absence of crowds and crowdiness, empty street corners, the anonymity of places and the facelessness of human figures, and a numbing monot-ony of an environment devoid of anything to puzzle, perplex or excite. The master plan of Brasilia eliminated chance encoun-ters from all places except the few specifically designed for purposeful gatherings. To make a rendezvous on the only planned 'forum', the enormous 'Square of Three Forces', was, according to the popular jibe, like agreeing to meet in the Gobi desert.

Brasilia was, perhaps, a space perfectly structured for the accommodation of homunculi, born and bred in test-tubes; for creatures patched together of administrative tasks and legal definitions. It was certainly (at least in its intention) a space perfectly transparent for those charged with the task of admin-istration and those who spelled out the content of such tasks.

Granted, it could be a perfectly structured place also for such ideal, imaginary residents, who would identify happiness with life free from problems, because it contained no ambivalent situations, no need to choose, no threat of risk and no chance of adventure. For all the rest it proved to be a space denuded of everything truly human – everything that fills life with meaning and makes it worth living.

Few urbanists consumed by the modernizing passion had been offered a field of action as vast as that entrusted to the imagination of Niemeyer. Most had to limit their flights of fancy (though not their ambition) to small-scale experiments with the city space: straightening up or fencing off here and there the devil-may-care, self-complacent chaos of city life, correcting one or another mistake or omission of history, cramming a little well-guarded niche of order into the extant universe of chance – but always with equally limited, far from comprehensive and in large part unpredictable consequences.

Agoraphobia and the renaissance of locality

Richard Sennett was the first analyst of contemporary city life to raise the alarm about the impending 'fall of the public man'. Many years ago he noticed the slow yet relentless curtailment of urban public space and the equally unstoppable withdrawal of city dwellers, from, and the subsequent devastation of, such pale shadows of the agora as escaped destruction.

In his later brilliant study of the 'uses of disorder',[6] Richard Sennett invokes the findings of Charles Abrams, Jane Jacobs, Marc Fried or Herbert Gans – researchers varied in temperament yet similar in their sensitivity to the experience of city life and investigative insight, and himself paints a frightening picture of the havoc visited upon 'the lives of real people for the sake of realizing some abstract plan of development or renewal'. Wherever the implementation of such plans was undertaken, the attempts to 'homogenize' the city space, to render it 'logical', 'functional' or 'legible', rebounded in the disintegration of protective nets woven of human bonds, in the psychically devastating experience of abandonment and loneliness – coupled with that of an inner void, horror of challenges which life may bring, and contrived illiteracy in the face of autonomous and responsible choices.

The pursuit of transparency had its awesome price. In an artifically conceived environment, calculated to secure anonymity and functional specialization of space, city dwellers faced an almost insoluble identity problem. The faceless monotony and clinical purity of the artificially construed space deprived them of the opportunity for meaning-negotiating and thus of the know-how needed to come to grips with that problem and to resolve it.

The lesson which planners could learn from the long chronicle of lofty dreams and abominable disasters which combine to form the history of modern architecture, is that the prime secret of a 'good city' is the chance it offers people to take responsibility for their acts 'in a historical unpredictable society', rather than 'in a dream world of harmony and predetermined order'. Whoever feels like dabbling in inventing city space while guided solely by the precepts of aesthetic harmony and reason, would be well advised to pause first and ponder that 'men can never become good simply by following the good orders or good plan of someone else.'

We may add that human responsibility, that ultimate and indispensable condition of morality of human intercourse, would find the perfectly designed space to be an infertile if not downright poisonous soil. Most certainly, it would not grow, let alone thrive, in a hygienically pure space, free of surprises, ambivalence and conflict. Only such people could face up to the fact of their responsibility who would have mastered the difficult art of acting under conditions of ambivalence and uncertainty, born of difference and variety. Morally mature persons are such human beings as grow 'to need the unknown, to feel incomplete without a certain anarchy in their lives' – who learn 'to love the "otherness" among them'.

The experience of American towns analysed by Sennett points to one well-nigh universal regularity: the suspicion against others, the intolerance of difference, the resentment of strangers, and the demands to separate and banish them, as well as the hysterical, paranoiac concern with 'law and order', all tend to climb to their highest pitch in the most uniform, the most racially, ethnically and class-wise segregated, homogeneous local communities.

No wonder: in such localities the support for the 'we-feeling' tends to be sought in the illusion of equality, secured by the monotonous similarity of everyone within sight. The guarantee of security tends to be adumbrated in the absence of differently thinking, differently acting and differently looking neighbours. Uniformity breeds conformity, and conformity's other face is intolerance. In a homogeneous locality it is exceedingly difficult to acquire the qualities of character and the skills needed to cope with human difference and situations of uncertainty; and in the absence of such skills and qualities it is all too easy to fear the other, simply for reason of being an-other – bizarre and different perhaps, but first and foremost unfamiliar, not-readily-comprehensible, not-fully-fathomed, unpredictable.

The city, built originally for the sake of security – to protect residents inside the city walls against malevolent invaders always coming from outside – in our times 'has become associated more with danger than with safety' – so says Nan Elin. In our postmodern times 'the fear factor has certainly grown, as indicated by the growth in locked car and house doors and security systems, the popularity of "gated" and "secure" communities for all age and income groups, and the increasing surveillance of public spaces, not to mention the unending reports of danger emitted by the mass media.'[7]

Contemporary fears, the typically 'urban fears', unlike those fears which led once to the construction of cities, focus on the 'enemy inside'. This kind of fear prompts less concern with the integrity and fortitude of the city *as a whole* – as a collective property and a collective warrant of individual safety – as it does with the isolation and fortification of one's own homestead *inside* the city. The walls built once around the city now criss-cross the city itself, and in a multitude of directions. Watched neighbourhoods, closely surveilled public spaces with selective admission, heavily armed guards at the gate and electronically operated doors – are all now aimed against the unwanted co-citizens, rather than foreign armies or highway robbers, marauders and other largely unknown dangers lying in ambush on the other side of the city gates.

Not togetherness, but avoidance and separation have become major survival strategies in the contemporary megalopolis. No more the question of loving or hating your neighbour. Keeping the neighbours at arm's length would take care of the dilemma and make the choice unnecessary; it staves off the occasions when the choice between love and hate needs to be made.

Is there life after Panopticon?

There are few allegorical images in social thought which match in their persuasive power that of the Panopticon. Michel Foucault used Jeremy Bentham's abortive project to great effect – as a metaphor for modern transformation, for the modern redeployment and redistribution of controlling powers. More insightfully than most of his contemporaries, Bentham saw through the variegated wrappings of controlling powers right to their major, and shared, task – which was to discipline through keeping the threat of punishment constantly real and tangible; and through the many names given to the fashions in which power was exercised to its basic, core strategy – which was to make subjects believe that at no moment could they hide from the ubiquitous eye of their superiors – and thus no misdemeanour, however secret, might go unpunished. In its 'ideal type', Panopticon would allow for no private space; at least for no *opaque* private space, no private space unsurveilled or worse still unsurveillable. In the city described in Zamiatin's *We*, everyone had a private home, but the walls of private homes were made of glass. In the city of Orwell's *Nineteen Eighty-Four*, everyone had a private TV set, but no one was ever allowed to switch it off, and no one could know at what particular moment the set was used by the broadcasters as a TV camera . . .

Panoptical techniques, as Foucault pointed out, played a crucial role in the passage from the locally based, self-surveilling and self-regulating mechanisms of integration made to the measure of the natural capacities of human eyes and ears, to the state-administered supra-local integration of territories much vaster than the reach of natural human faculties. That latter function called for the asymmetricality of surveillance, for professional watchers, and for such reorganization of space as would enable the watchers to do their job, and would make the watched aware that the job was being done, and could be done, at any moment. All such demands came close to being met in full in major discipline-drilling institutions of 'classic' modernity – above all in industrial plants and mass conscript armies, both endowed with well-nigh universal catchment-areas.

Being a near-perfect metaphor for the crucial facets of modernization of power and control, the image of Panopticon may, however, dwell too heavily on the sociological imagination, thus preventing, rather than facilitating, the perception of the nature of present change. To the detriment of analysis, we are naturally inclined to spy out in the contemporary arrangements of power a new and improved rendition of old and basically unchanged panoptical techniques. We tend to overlook the fact that the majority of the population has no longer either the need or the chance to be dragged through the drilling fields of yore. We also tend to forget the peculiar challenges of the modernizing process which made panoptical strategies both feasible and attractive. Today's challenges are different, and in the task of facing many of them, perhaps the most important among them, the orthodox panoptical strategies, if pursued with unabated vigour, would most certainly prove irrelevant or downright counter-productive.

In his brilliant essay on the electronic database as an updated cyberspatial version of the Panopticon, Mark Poster proposes that 'our bodies are hooked into the networks, the databases, the information highways' – and thus all these information-storing sites where our bodies are, so to speak, 'tied down informatically', 'no longer provide a refuge from observation or a bastion around which one can draw a line of resistance'. The storage of massive quantities of data, amplified with every use of a credit card and virtually each act of purchase, results according to Poster in a 'superpanopticon' – but a Panopticon with a difference: the surveilled, supplying the data for storage, are prime – and *willing* – factors in the surveillance. It is true that the amount of stored information about them makes people worry; *Time* magazine found that 70–80 per cent of its readers were 'very/somewhat concerned' in 1991 – more by the information collected by the government and credit and insurance companies, less by data stored by employers, banks and marketing firms. In view of all that, Poster wonders why 'database anxiety has not as yet developed into an issue of national political prominence'.[8]

One wonders, though, why should one wonder . . . Under closer scrutiny, most of the apparent similarity between Foucault's Panopticon and contemporary databases seems fairly superficial. The Panopticon's main purpose was to instill discipline and to impose a uniform pattern on the behaviour of its inmates; the Panopticon was first and foremost a weapon against difference, choice and variety. No such target is set for the database and its potential uses. Quite the opposite – it is the credit and marketing companies which are the main movers and users behind the database, and what they seek is to make sure that the records confirm the 'credibility' of the people on record – their reliability as clients and *choosers*, and that those incapable of choice are sifted out before damage is done or resources wasted; indeed, *being included* in the database is the prime condition of 'creditworthiness' and so is the means of access to 'the best game in town'. The Panopticon ensnared its inmates as producers and/or soldiers, of whom routine and monotonous conduct was expected and demanded; the database puts on record the reliable and trustworthy consumers – and sifts out all the rest who are not to be trusted with the capacity for the consumer game, simply by the fact of there being nothing in their life-pursuits to record. The Panopticon's main function was to make sure that no one could *escape* beyond the closely guarded space; the database's main function is to make sure that no intruder can *enter* it under false pretences and without proper credentials. The more information about you the database contains, the more freely you can move.

The database is an instrument of selection, separation and exclusion. It keeps the globals in the sieve and washes out the locals. Certain people it admits to the exterritorial cyberspace, making them feel at home wherever they go and welcome wherever they arrive; certain others it deprives of passports and transit visas and stops from roaming the places reserved for the residents of cyberspace. But the latter effect is subsidiary and complementary to the former. Unlike the Panopticon, the database is a vehicle of mobility, not the fetters keeping people in place.

One can also consider the historical fate of the Panopticon from a different perspective. In a memorable phrase coined by Thomas Mathiesen, the introduction of panoptical power represented a fundamental transformation *from a situation where the many watch the few to a situation where the few watch the many*.[9] In the exercise of power, surveillance replaced the spectacle. In pre-modern times, power used to impress itself upon the *populus* through letting the commoners watch in awe, fear and admiration its own pomp, wealth and splendour. Now the new modern power preferred to stay in the shadows, watching its subjects rather than being watched by them. Mathiesen takes Foucault to task for not giving due attention to the parallel modern process: the development of new techniques of power, consisting – on the contrary – in the many (as many as never before in history) watching the few. He means, of course, the rise and rise of mass media – television more than any other – that leads to the creation, alongside the Panopticon, of another power mechanism which, coining another apt phrase, he dubs the *Synopticon*.

Consider, though, the following. The Panopticon, even when it was universal in its application and when the institutions following its principles embraced the bulk of the population, was by its nature a local establishment: both the condition and the effects of panoptical institution was *immobilization* of its subjects – surveillance was there to stave off escape or at least to prevent autonomous, contingent and erratic movements. The Synopticon is in its nature global; the act of watching unties the watchers from their locality – transports them at least spiritually into cyberspace, in which distance no longer matters, even if bodily they remain in place. It does not matter any more if the targets of the Synopticon, transformed now from the *watched* into the *watchers*, move around or stay in place. Wherever they may be and wherever they may go, they may – and they do – link into the exterritorial web which makes the many watch the few. The Panopticon *forced* people into the position where they could be watched. The Synopticon needs no coercion – it *seduces* people into watching. And the few whom the watchers watch are tightly selected. In Mathiesen's words,

we know about who are allowed to enter the media from the outside to express their views. A number of international and Norwegian studies have shown that they systematically belong to *the institutional elites.* Those who are allowed to enter are systematically men – not women – from the higher social strata, with power in political life, private industry and public bureaucracy.

The widely eulogized 'interactivity' of the new media is a gross exaggeration; one should rather speak of 'an interactive one-way medium'. Contrary to what academics, themselves members of the new global elite, tend to believe, the Internet and Web are not for anyone and unlikely ever to become open to universal use. Even those who get access are allowed to make their choices within the frame set by the suppliers, who invite them 'to spend time and money choosing between and in the numerous packages they offer'. As for the rest, left with the network of satellite or cable television with not as much as a pretention to symmetry between the two sides of the screen – pure and unalloyed watching is their lot. And what is it that they watch?

The many watch the few. The few who are watched are the celebrities. They may come from the world of politics, of sport, of science or showbusiness, or just be celebrated information specialists. Wherever they come from, though, all displayed celebrities put on display the world of celebrities – a world whose main distinctive feature is precisely the quality of being watched – by many, and in all corners of the globe: of being global in their capacity of being watched. Whatever they speak about when on air, they convey the message of a total way of life. *Their* life, their *way of life.* Asking about the impact which that message may have on the watchers 'is less like asking about preconceived fears and hopes and more like asking about the 'effects' of Christianity on one's view of the world, or – as the Chinese *had* asked – of Confucianism on public morality.'[10]

In the Panopticon, some selected locals watched other locals (and before the advent of the Panopticon, ordinary rank-and-file locals watched the selected ones among them). In the Synopticon, locals watch the globals. The authority of the latter is secured by their very remoteness; the globals are literally 'out of this world', but their hovering above the worlds of the local is much more, daily and obtrusively, visible than that of the angels who once hovered over the Christian world: simultaneously inaccessible and within sight, lofty and mundane, infinitely superior yet setting a shining example for all the inferiors to follow or to dream of following; admired and coveted at the same time – a royalty that guides instead of ruling.

Segregated and separated on earth, the locals meet the globals through the regular televised broadcasts of heaven. The echoes of the encounter reverberate globally, stifling all local sounds yet reflected by the local walls, whose prison-like impenetrable solidity is thereby revealed and reinforced.

3

After the Nation-state – What?

'In an earlier generation, social policy was based on the belief that nations, and within nations cities, could control their fortunes; now, a divide is opening between polity and economy' – observes Richard Sennett.[1]

With the overall speed of movement gathering momentum – with time/space as such, as David Harvey points out, 'compressing' – some objects move faster than others. 'The economy' – capital, which means money and other resources needed to get things done, to make more money and more things yet – moves fast; enough to keep permanently a step ahead of any (territorial, as ever) polity which may try to contain and redirect its travels. in this case, at least, the reduction of travel time to zero leads to a new quality: to a total annihilation of spatial constraints, or rather to the total 'overcoming of gravity'. Whatever moves with the speed approaching the velocity of the electronic signal, is practically free from constraints related to the territory inside which it originated, towards which it is aimed or through which it passes on the way.

A recent commentary by Martin Woollacott grasps well the consequences of that emancipation:

The Swedish-Swiss conglomerate Asea Brown Boveri announced it would be cutting its West European work force by 57,000, while creating other jobs in Asia. Electrolux followed with the announcement that it will cut its global work force by 11 per cent, with most of the cuts in Europe and North America. Pilkington Glass also announced significant cuts. In just ten days, three European firms had cut jobs on a scale large enough to be compared with the numbers mentioned in the new French and British governments' proposals on job creation . . .

Germany, notoriously, has lost 1 million jobs in five years, and its companies are busy building plants in Eastern Europe, Asia, and Latin America. If West European industry is massively relocating outside Western Europe, then all these arguments about the best government approach to unemployment would have to be seen as of limited relevance.[2]

Balancing the books of what once seemed to be the indispensable setting for all economic thinking – the *Nationalökonomie* – is becoming more and more an actuarial fiction. As Vincent Cable points out in his recent *Demos* pamphlet – 'it is no longer obvious what it means to describe the Midland Bank or ICL as British (or for that matter companies like British Petroleum, British Airways, British Gas or British Telecom) . . . In a world where capital has no fixed abode and financial flows are largely beyond the control of national governments, many of the levers of economic policy no longer work.'[3] And Alberto Melucci suggests that the rapidly growing influence of supranational – 'planetary' – organizations 'has had the effect of both accelerating the exclusion of weak areas and of creating new channels for the allocation of resources, removed, at least in part, from the control of the various national states'.[4]

In the words of G. H. von Wright, the 'nation-state, it seems, is eroding or perhaps "withering away". The eroding forces are *transnational*.' Since nation-states remain the sole frame for book-balancing and the sole sources of effective political initiative, the 'transnationality' of eroding forces puts them outside the realm of deliberate, purposeful and potentially rational action. As everything that elides such action, such forces, their shapes and actions are blurred in the mist of mystery; they are objects of guesses rather than reliable analysis. As von Wright puts it,

> The moulding forces of transnational character are largely anonymous and therefore difficult to identify. They do not form a unified system or order. They are an agglomeration of systems manipulated by largely 'invisible' actors . . . [there is no] unity or purposeful co-ordination of the forces in question . . . '[M]arket' is not a bargaining interaction of competing forces so much as the pull and push of manipulated demands, artificially created needs, and desire for quick profit.[5]

All this surrounds the ongoing process of the 'withering away' of nation-states with an aura of a natural catastrophe. Its causes are not fully understood; it cannot be exactly predicted even if the causes are known; and it certainly cannot be prevented from happening even if predicted. The feeling of unease, an expectable response to a situation without obvious levers of control, has been pointedly and incisively captured in the title of Kenneth Jowitt's book – *The New World Disorder*. Throughout the modern era we have grown used to the idea that order is tantamount to 'being in control'. It is this assumption – whether well-founded or merely illusionary – of 'being in control' which we miss most.

The present-day 'new world disorder' cannot be explained away merely by the circumstance which constitutes the most immediate and obvious reason to feel at a loss and aghast: namely, by 'the morning-after' confusion following the abrupt end of the Great Schism and the sudden collapse of the power-block political routine – even if it was indeed that collapse which triggered the 'new disorder' alert. The image of global disorder reflects, rather, the new awareness (facilitated, but not necessarily caused, by the abrupt demise of block politics) of the essentially elemental and contingent nature of the things which previously seemed to be tightly controlled or at least 'technically controllable'.

Before the collapse of the Communist block, the contingent, erratic and wayward nature of the global state of affairs was not so much non-existent, as it was barred from sight by the all-energy-and-thought-consuming day-to-day reproduction of the balance between the world powers. By dividing the world, power politics conjured up the image of totality. Our shared world was made whole by assigning to each nook and cranny of the globe its significance in the 'global order of things' – to wit, in the two power-camps' conflict and the meticulously guarded, though forever precarious, equilibrium. The world was a totality in as far as there was nothing in it which could escape such significance, and so nothing could be indifferent from the point of view of the balance between the two powers which appropriated a considerable part of the world and cast the rest in the shadow of that appropriation. Everything in the world had a meaning, and that meaning emanated from a split, yet single centre – from the two enormous power blocks locked up, riveted and glued to each other in an all-out combat. With the Great Schism out of the way, the world does not look a totality anymore; it looks rather like a field of scattered and disparate forces, congealing in places difficult to predict and gathering momentum which no one really knows how to arrest.

To put it in a nutshell: *no one seems now to be in control.* Worse still – it is not clear what 'being in control' could, under the circumstances, be like. As before, all ordering initiatives and actions are local and issue-oriented; but there is no longer a locality arrogant enough to pronounce for mankind as a whole, or to be listened to and obeyed by mankind when making the pronouncements. Neither is there a single issue which could grasp and telescope the totality of global affairs while commanding global consent.

Universalizing – or being globalized?

It is this novel and uncomfortable perception of 'things getting out of hand' which has been articulated (with little benefit to intellectual clarity) in the currently fashionable concept of *globalization*. The deepest meaning conveyed by the idea of globalization is that of the indeterminate, unruly and self-propelled character of world affairs; the absence of a centre, of a controlling desk, of a board of directors, of a managerial office. Globalization is Jowitt's 'new world disorder' under another name.

This trait, undetachable from the image of globalization, sets it radically apart from another idea which it ostensibly replaced, that of 'universalization' – once constitutive of the modern discourse of global affairs, but by now fallen into disuse, rarely heard of, perhaps even by and large forgotten by anyone except philosophers.

Just like the concepts of 'civilization', 'development', 'convergence', 'consensus' and many other key terms of early- and classic-modern thinking, the idea of 'universalization' conveyed the hope, the intention, and the determination of order-making; on top of what the other kindred terms signalled, it meant a *universal* order – the order-*making* on a universal, truly global scale. Like the other concepts, the idea of universalization was coined on the rising tide of the modern powers' resourcefulness and the modern intellect's ambitions. The entire family of concepts announced in unison the will to make the world different from what it had been and better than it had been, and expand the change and the improvement to a global, species-wide dimension. By the same token, it declared the intention to make similar the life conditions of everyone and everywhere, and so everybody's life chances; perhaps even make them equal.

Nothing of that has been left in the meaning of globalization, as shaped by the present discourse. The new term refers primarily to the global *effects*, notoriously unintended and unanticipated, rather than to global *initiatives* and *undertakings*.

Yes, it says: our actions may have, and often do have, global effects; but no – we do not have, nor do we know well how to obtain, the means to plan and execute actions globally. 'Globalization' is not about what we all, or at least the most resourceful and enterprising among us, wish or hope *to do*. It is about *what is happening to us all*. The idea of 'globalization' explicitly refers to von Wright's 'anonymous forces', operating in the vast – foggy and slushy, impassable and untamable – 'no man's land', stretching beyond the reach of the design-and-action capacity of anybody's in particular.

How has it come about that this vast expanse of man-made wilderness (not the 'natural' wilderness which modernity set out to conquer and tame; but, to paraphrase Anthony Giddens's felicitous phrase, a '*manufactured* jungle' – the post-domestication wilderness, one that emerged *after* the conquest, and as its result) has sprung into vision? And why did it acquire that formidable power of obstinacy and resilience which since Durkheim is taken to be the defining mark of 'hard reality'?

A plausible explanation is the growing experience of weakness, indeed of impotence, of the habitual, taken-for-granted ordering agencies.

Among the latter, pride of place throughout the modern era belonged to the state. (One is tempted to say: to the *territorial* state, but the ideas of the state and of 'territorial sovereignty' had become in modern practice and theory synonymous, and thus the phrase 'territorial state' became pleonastic.) The meaning of 'the state' has been precisely that of an agency claiming the legitimate right and boasting sufficient resources to set up and enforce the rules and norms binding the run of affairs within a certain territory; the rules and norms hoped and expected to turn contingency into determination, ambivalence into *Eindeutigkeit,* randomness into regularity – in short, the primeval forest into a carefully plotted garden, chaos into order.

To order a certain section of the world came to mean: to set up a state endowed with the sovereignty to do just that. It also necessarily meant the ambition to enforce a certain model of preferred order at the expense of other, competitive, models. This could be implemented solely through acquiring the vehicle of the state, or by capturing the driving seat of the existing one.

Max Weber defined the state as the agency claiming monopoly over the means of coercion and over their use inside its sovereign territory. Cornelius Castoriadis warns against the widespread habit of confusing the state with social power as such: 'State', he insists, refers to a particular way of distributing and condensing social power, precisely with the enhanced ability 'to order' in mind. 'The State', says Castoriadis, 'is an entity *separated* from the collectivity and instituted in such a manner as to secure the permanence of that separation.' One should reserve the name of 'the State' 'for such cases when it is instituted in the form of the *State Apparatus* – which implies a separate 'bureaucracy', civil, clerical or military, even if only rudimentary: in other words, a hierarchical organization with delimited area of competence.'[6]

Let us point out, though, that such 'separation of social power from collectivity' was by no means a chance event, one of the vagaries of history. The task of order-making requires huge and continuous efforts of creaming-off, shifting and condensing social power, which in turn call for considerable resources that *only* the state, in the form of a hierarchical bureaucratic apparatus, is able to muster, focus and deploy. Of necessity, the legislative and executive sovereignty of the modern state was perched on the 'tripod' of military, economic and cultural sovereignties; in other words, on the state's dominion over the resources once deployed by the diffuse foci of social power, but now all needed to sustain the institution and maintenance of the state-administered order. An effective order-making capacity was unthinkable unless supported by the ability to defend effectively the territory against challenges of other models of order, both from outside and inside the realm; by the ability to balance the books of the *Nationalökonomie*; and the ability to muster enough cultural resources to sustain the state's identity and distinctiveness through distinctive identity of its subjects.

Only a few populations aspiring to state sovereignty of their own were large and resourceful enough to pass such a demanding test, and thus to contemplate sovereignty and statehood as a *realistic* prospect. The times when the ordering job was undertaken and performed primarily, perhaps solely, through the agency of sovereign states, were for that reason the times of relatively few states. By the same token, the establishment of any sovereign state required as a rule the suppression of state-formative ambitions of many lesser populations – undermining or expropriating however little they might have possessed of inchoate military capacity, economic self-sufficiency and cultural distinctiveness.

Under such circumstances, the 'global scene' was the theatre of *inter-state* politics, which – through armed conflicts, bargaining or both – aimed first and foremost at the drawing and preserving ('internationally guaranteeing') of the boundaries that set apart and enclosed the territory of each state's legislative and executive sovereignty. 'Global politics', in as far as the foreign politics of sovereign states had anything like global horizons, concerned itself mostly with sustaining the principle of full and uncontested sovereignty of each state over its territory, with the effacing of the few 'blank spots' remaining on the world map, and fighting off the danger of ambivalence arising from occasional overlapping of sovereignties or from outstanding territorial claims. In an oblique, yet emphatic tribute to that vision, the main decision taken unanimously at the first, founding session of the Organisation of African Unity, was to proclaim sacrosanct and unchangeable all new state boundaries – by common agreement totally artificial products of the colonial legacy. The image of the 'global order' boiled down, in short, to the sum-total of a number of local orders, each effectively maintained and efficiently policed by one, and one only, territorial state. All states were expected to rally to the defence of one another's policing rights.

Superimposed upon that parcelled-out world of sovereign states for almost half a century and until a few years ago were two power blocks. Each of the two blocks promoted a growing degree of co-ordination between the state-managed orders inside the realm of its respective 'meta-sovereignty', based on the assumption of each singular state's military, economic and cultural insufficiency. Gradually yet relentlessly, a new principle was promoted – in political practice faster than in political theory – of *supra*-state integration. The 'global scene' was seen increasingly as the theatre of coexistence and competition between *groups of states*, rather than between the states themselves.

The Bandung initiative to establish the incongruous 'non-block block', and the ensuing, recurrent efforts of alignment undertaken by non-aligned states, was an oblique acknowledgement of that new principle. That initiative was, however, consistently and effectively sapped by the two super-blocks, which stayed unanimous on at least one point: they both treated the rest of the world as the twentieth-century equivalent of the 'blank spots' of the nineteenth-century state-building and state-enclosure race. Non-alignment, refusal to join either one or the other of the two super-blocks, obstinate attachment to the old-fashioned and increasingly obsolete principle of supreme sovereignty vested with the state – was seen as the blocks-era equivalent of that 'no man's land' ambivalence which was fought off tooth and nail, competitively yet in unison, by modern states at their formative stage.

The political superstructure of the Great Schism era barred from sight the deeper, and – as it has now transpired – more seminal and lasting departures in the mechanism of order-making. The change affected above all the role of the state. All three legs of the 'sovereignty tripod' have been broken beyond repair. The military, economic and cultural self-sufficiency, indeed self-sustainability, of the state – any state – ceased to be a viable prospect. In order to retain their law-and-order policing ability, states had to seek alliances and voluntarily surrender ever larger chunks of their sovereignty. And when the curtain was eventually torn apart, it uncovered an unfamiliar scene, populated by bizarre characters.

There were now states which – far from being forced to give up their sovereign rights – actively and keenly sought to surrender them, and begged for their sovereignty to be taken away and dissolved in the supra-state formations. There were unheard-of or forgotten local 'ethnicities' – long deceased yet born again, or never previously heard of but now duly invented – often too small, hard-up and inept to pass any of the traditional tests of sovereignty, yet nevertheless demanding states of their own, states with the full trappings of political sovereignty and the right to legislate and police order on their own territory. There were old or new nations escaping the federalist cages in which they had been incarcerated by the now extinct Communist super-power against their will – but only to use their newly acquired decision-making freedom to pursue the dissolution of their political, economic and military independence in the European Market and NATO alliance.[7] The new chance, contained in the ignoring of the stern and demanding conditions of statehood, has found its acknowledgement in the dozens of 'new nations' rushing to install their offices inside the already overcrowded UN building, not originally expected to accommodate such huge numbers of 'equals'.

Paradoxically, it was the *demise* of state sovereignty, not its triumph, that made the idea of statehood so tremendously popular. In the caustic estimate of Eric Hobsbawm, once the Seychelles can have a vote in the UN as good as Japan's 'the majority of the members of the UN is soon likely to consist of the late twentieth-century (republican) equivalents to Saxe-Coburg-Gotha and Schwarzburg-Sonderhausen.'[8]

The new expropriation: this time, of the state

Indeed, the new states, just like the longer-living ones in their present condition, are no longer expected to perform most of the functions once seen as the *raison d'être* of the nation-state bureaucracies. The function most conspicuous for having been dropped by the orthodox state, or torn out of its hands, is the maintenance of that 'dynamic equilibrium' which Castoriadis describes as 'approximate equality between the rhythms of the growth of consumption and the elevation of productivity' – the task which led the sovereign states at various times to impose intermittently import or export bans, customs barriers, or state-managed Keynes-style stimulation of internal demand.[9] Any control of such 'dynamic equilibrium' is now beyond the means, and indeed beyond the ambitions, of the overwhelming majority of the otherwise sovereign (in the strictly order-policing sense) states. The very distinction between the internal and global market, or more generally between the 'inside' and the 'outside' of the state, is exceedingly difficult to maintain in any but the most narrow, 'territory and population policing' sense.

All three legs of the sovereignty tripod have now been shattered. Arguably, the crushing of the economic leg has been most seminal. No longer capable of balancing the books while guided solely by the politically articulated interests of the population within their realm of political sovereignty, the nation-states turn more and more into the executors and plenipotentiaries of forces which they have no hope of controlling politically. In the incisive verdict of the radical Latin-American political analyst, thanks to the new 'porousness' of all allegedly 'national' economies, and to the ephemerality, elusiveness and non-territoriality of the space in which they operate, global financial markets 'impose their laws and precepts on the planet. The "globalization" is nothing more than a totalitarian extension of their logic on all aspects of life.' States have not enough resources or freedom of manoeuvre to withstand the pressure – for the simple reason that 'a few minutes is enough for enterprises and the states themselves to collapse':

> In the cabaret of globalization, the state goes through a strip-tease and by the end of the performance it is left with the bare necessities only: its powers of repression. With its material basis destroyed, its sovereignty and independence annulled, its political class effaced, the nation-state becomes a simple security service for the mega-companies . . .
>
> The new masters of the world have no need to govern directly. National governments are charged with the task of administering affairs on their behalf.[10]

Due to the unqualified and unstoppable spread of free trade rules, and above all the free movement of capital and finances, the 'economy' is progressively exempt from political control; indeed, the prime meaning conveyed by the term 'economy' is 'the area of the non-political'. Whatever has been left of politics is expected to be dealt with, as in the good old days, by the state – but whatever is concerned with the economic life the state is not allowed to touch: any attempt in this direction would be met with prompt and furious punitive action from the world markets. The economic impotence of the state would once more be blatantly displayed to the horror of its current governing team. According to the calculations of René Passat,[11] purely speculative inter-currency financial transactions reach a total volume of $1,300 billion a day – fifty times greater than the volume of commercial exchanges and almost equal to the total of $1,500 billion to which all the reserves of all the 'national banks' of the world amount. 'No state', Passat concludes, 'can therefore resist for more than a few days the speculative pressures of the "markets".'

The sole economic task which the state is allowed and expected to handle is to secure 'the equilibrated budget' by policing and keeping in check the local pressures for more vigorous state intervention in the running of businesses and for the defence of the population from the more sinister consequences of market anarchy. As Jean-Paul Fitoussi has recently pointed out,

> Such a programme, though, cannot be implemented unless in one way or another the economy is taken out from the field of politics. A ministry of finances remains certainly a necessary evil, but ideally one would dispose of the ministry of economic affairs (that is, of the governing of economy). In other words, the government should be deprived of its responsibility for macro-economic policy.[12]

Contrary to oft-repeated (yet no more true for that reason) opinions, there is neither logical nor pragmatic contradiction between the new exterritoriality of capital (complete in the case of finances, nearly complete in the case of trade, and well advanced in the case of industrial production) and the new proliferation of feeble and impotent sovereign states. The rush to carve out ever new and ever weaker and less resourceful 'politically independent' territorial entities does not go against the grain of the globalizing economic tendencies; political fragmentation is not a 'spoke in the wheel' of the emergent 'world society', bonded by the free circulation of information. On the contrary – there seems to be an intimate kinship, mutual conditioning and reciprocal reinforcement between the 'globalization' of all aspects of the economy and the renewed emphasis on the 'territorial principle'.

For their liberty of movement and for their unconstrained freedom to pursue their ends, global finance, trade and the information industry depend on the political fragmentation – the *morcellement* – of the world scene. They have all, one may say, developed vested interests in 'weak states' – that is, in such states as are *weak* but nevertheless *remain states*. Deliberately or subconsciously, such inter-state, supra-local institutions as have been brought into being and are allowed to act with the consent of global capital, exert co-ordinated pressures on all member or independent states to destroy systematically everything which could stem or slow down the free movement of capital and limit market liberty. Throwing wide open the gates and abandoning any thought of autonomous economic policy is the preliminary, and meekly complied with, condition of eligibility for financial assistance from world banks and monetary funds. Weak states is precisely what the New World Order, all too often looking suspiciously like a new world *disorder*, needs to sustain and reproduce itself. Weak, quasi-states can be easily reduced to the (useful) role of local police precincts, securing a modicum of order required for the conduct of business, but need not be feared as effective brakes on the global companies' freedom.

The separation of economy from politics and the exemption of the first from the regulatory intervention of the second, resulting in the disempowerment of politics as an effective agency, augurs much more than just a shift in the distribution of social power. As Claus Offe points out, the political agency as such – 'the capacity to make collectively binding choices and to carry them out' – has become problematic. 'Instead of asking what is to be done, we might more fruitfully explore whether there is anybody capable of doing whatever needs to be done.' Since 'borders have become penetrable' (highly selectively, to be sure), 'sovereignties have become nominal, power anonymous, and its locus empty'. We are still far from the ultimate destination; the process goes on, seemingly unstoppably. 'The dominant pattern might be described as "releasing the brakes": deregulation, liberalization, flexibility, increasing fluidity, and facilitating the transactions on the financial real estate and labour markets, easing the tax burden, etc.'[13] The more consistently this pattern is applied, the less power remains in the hands of the agency which promotes it; and less can the increasingly resourceless agency retreat from applying it, if it so wished or if it was pressed to do so.

One of the most seminal consequences of the new global freedom of movement is that it becomes increasingly difficult, perhaps altogether impossible, to re-forge social issues into effective collective action.

The global hierarchy of mobility

Let us recall once more what Michel Crozier pointed out many years ago in his trail-blazing study of *The Bureaucratic Phenomenon*: all dominance consists in the pursuit of an essentially similar strategy – to leave as much leeway and freedom of manoeuvre to the dominant, while imposing the strictest possible constraints on the decisional freedom of the dominated side.

This strategy was once successfully applied by state governments, which now, however, find themselves on its receiving end. It is now the conduct of the 'markets' – primarily, world finances – which is the main source of surprise and uncertainty. It is not difficult to see therefore that the replacement of territorial 'weak states' by some sort of global legislative and policing powers would be detrimental to the interests of 'world markets'. And so it is easy to suspect that, far from acting at cross-purposes and being at war with each other, political fragmentation and economic globalization are close allies and fellow conspirators.

Integration and parcelling out, globalization and territorialization, are *mutually complementary processes*. More precisely, they are two sides of the same process: that of the world-wide redistribution of sovereignty, power and the freedom to act, triggered (though by no means determined) by the radical leap in the technology of speed. The coincidence and intertwining of synthesis and dissipation, integration and decomposition are anything but accidental; even less are they rectifiable.

It is because of this coincidence and intertwining of the two apparently opposite tendencies, both set in motion by the divisive impact of the new freedom of movement, that the so-called 'globalizing' processes rebound in the redistribution of privileges and deprivations, of wealth and poverty, of resources and impotence, of power and powerlessness, of freedom and constraint. We witness today the process of a world-wide *restratification*, in the course of which a new socio-cultural hierarchy, a world-wide scale, is put together.

The quasi-sovereignties, territorial divisions and segregations of identities which the globalization of markets and information promotes and renders 'a must', do not reflect diversity of equal partners. What is a free choice for some descends as cruel fate upon others. And since those 'others' tend to grow unstoppably in numbers and sink ever deeper into despair born of a prospectless existence, one will be well advised to speak of *'glocalization'* (Roland Robertson's apt term, exposing the unbreakable unity between 'globalizing' and 'localizing' pressures – a phenomenon glossed over in the one-sided concept of globalization), and to define it mostly as the process of the concentration of capital, finance and all other resources of choice and effective action, but also – perhaps above all – of *the concentration of freedom* to move and to act (two freedoms which for all practical purposes have become synonymous).

Commenting on the findings of the UN's latest *Human Development Report*, that the total wealth of the top 358 'global billionaires' equals the combined incomes of 2.3 billion poorest people (45 per cent of the world's population), Victor Keegan[14] called the present reshuffling of the world resources 'a new form of highway robbery'. Indeed, only 22 per cent of global *wealth* belongs to the so-called 'developing countries', which account for about 80 per cent of the world population. And yet this is by no means the limit the present polarization is likely to reach, since the share of the global *income* currently apportioned to the poor is smaller still: in 1991, 85 per cent of the world's population received only 15 per cent of its income. No wonder that in the abysmally meagre 2.3 per cent of global wealth owned by 20 per cent of the poorest countries thirty years ago has fallen by now still further, to 1.4 per cent.

Also the global network of communication, acclaimed as the gateway to a new and unheard-of freedom, and above all as the technological foundation of imminent equality, is clearly very selectively used; a narrow cleft in the thick wall, rather than a gate. Few (and fewer) people get the passes entitling them to go through. 'All computers do for the Third World these days is to chronicle their decline more efficiently,' says Keegan. And concludes: 'If (as one American critic observed) the 358 decided to keep $5 million or so each, to tide themselves over, and give the rest away, they could virtually double the annual incomes of nearly half the people on Earth. And pigs would fly.'

In the words of John Kavanagh of the Washington Institute of Policy Research,

> Globalization has given more opportunities for the extremely wealthy to make money more quickly. These individuals have utilized the latest technology to move large sums of money around the globe extremely quickly and speculate ever more efficiently.
>
> Unfortunately, the technology makes no impact on the lives of the world poor. In fact, globalization is a paradox: while it is very beneficial to a very few, it leaves out or marginalizes two-thirds of the world's population.[15]

As the folklore of the new generation of 'enlightened classes', gestated in the new, brave and monetarist world of nomadic capital, would have it, opening up sluices and dynamiting all state-maintained dams will make the world a free place for everybody. According to such folkloristic beliefs, freedom (of trade and capital mobility, first and foremost) is the hothouse in which wealth would grow faster than ever before; and once the wealth is multiplied, there will be more of it for everybody.

The poor of the world – whether old or new, hereditary or computer-made – would hardly recognize their plight in this folkloristic fiction. The media are the message, and the media through which the establishment of the world-wide market is being perpetrated do not facilitate, but, on the contrary, preclude the promised 'trickle-down' effect. New fortunes are born, sprout and flourish in the virtual reality, tightly isolated from the old-fashioned rough-and-ready realities of the poor. The creation of wealth is on the way to finally emancipating itself from its perennial – constraining and vexing – connections with making things, processing materials, creating jobs and managing people. The old rich needed the poor to make and keep them rich. That dependency at all times mitigated the conflict of interest and prompted some effort, however tenuous, to care. The new rich do not need the poor any more. At long last the bliss of ultimate freedom is nigh.

The lie of the free-trade promise is well covered up; the connection between the growing misery and desperation of the 'grounded' many and the new freedoms of the mobile few is difficult to spot in the reports coming from the lands cast on the receiving side of 'glocalization'. It seems, on the contrary, that the two phenomena belong to different worlds, each having its own, sharply distinct causes. One would never guess from the reports that the fast enrichment and fast impoverishment stem from the same root, that the 'grounding' of the miserable is as legitimate outcome of the 'glocalizing' pressures as are the new sky's-the-limit freedoms of the successful (as one would never guess from sociological analyses of the holocaust and other genocides that they are equally 'at home' in modern society as are economic, technological, scientific and standard-of-living progress).

As Ryszard Kapuściński, one of the most formidable chronographers of contemporary living, has recently explained, that effective cover-up is achieved by three inter-connected expedients consistently applied by the media which preside over the occasional, carnival-like outbursts of public interest in the plight of the 'poor of the world'.[16]

First, the news of a famine – arguably the last remaining reason for breaking the day-by-day indifference – as a rule comes coupled with the emphatic reminder that the same distant lands where people 'as seen on TV' die of famine and disease, are the birthplace of 'Asian tigers', the exemplary beneficiaries of the new imaginative and brave way of getting things done. It does not matter that all the 'tigers' together embrace no more than 1 per cent of the population of Asia alone. They are assumed to demonstrate what was to be proved – that the sorry plight of the hungry and indolent is their *sui generis* choice: alternatives are available, and within reach – but not taken for the lack of industry or resolve. The underlying message is that the poor themselves bear responsibility for their fate; that they could, as the 'tigers' did, choose easy prey has nothing to do with the tigers' appetites.

Second, the news is so scripted and edited as to reduce the problem of poverty and deprivation to the question of hunger alone. This stratagem achieves two effects in one go: the real scale of poverty is played down (800 million people are permanently undernourished, but something like 4 billion – two-thirds of the world population – live in poverty), and the task ahead is limited to finding food for the hungry. But, as Kapuściński points out, such presentation of the problem of poverty (as examplified by one of *The Economist*'s recent issues analysing world poverty under the heading 'How to feed the world') 'terribly degrades, virtually denies full humanity to people whom we want, allegedly, to help'. What the equation 'poverty = hunger' conceals are many other and complex aspects of poverty – 'horrible living and housing conditions, illness, illiteracy, aggression, falling apart families, weakening of social bonds, lack of future and non-productiveness' – afflictions which cannot be cured with high-protein biscuits and powdered milk. Kapuściński remembers wandering through African townships and villages and meeting children 'who begged me not for bread, water, chocolate or toys, but a ballpoint, since they went to school and had nothing to write their lessons with'.

Let us add that all associations of the horrid pictures of famine, as presented by the media, with the destruction of work and work-places (that is, with the global causes of local poverty) are carefully avoided. People are shown together with their hunger – but however the viewers strain their eyes, they will not see a single work-tool, plot of arable land or head of cattle in the picture – and one hears no reference to them. As if there was no connection between the emptiness of the routine 'get up and do something' exhortations addressed to the poor in a world which needs no more labour, certainly not in the lands where people on the screen starve, and the plight of people offered as a carnival-like, 'charity fair' outlet for a pent-up moral impulse. The riches are global, the misery is local – but there is no causal link between the two; not in the spectacle of the fed and the feeding, anyway.

Victor Hugo let Enjolras, one of his characters, wistfully exclaim a moment before his death on one of the many nineteenth-century barricades: 'The twentieth century will be happy.' As it happened – René Passet comments – 'the same technologies of the immaterial which sustained that promise entail simultaneously its denial', particularly when 'coupled with the frantic policy of planetary liberalization of capital exchanges and movements'. Technologies which effectively do away with time and space need little time to denude and impoverish space. They render capital truly global; they make all those who can neither follow nor arrest capital's new nomadic habits helplessly watch their livelihood fading and vanishing and wonder from where the blight might have come. The global travels of financial resources are perhaps as immaterial as the electronic network they travel – but the local traces of their journeys are painfully tangible and real: 'qualitative depopulation', destruction of local economies once capable of sustaining their inhabitants, the exclusion of the millions incapable of being absorbed by the new global economy.

Third, the spectacle of disasters, as presented by the media, also support and reinforce the ordinary, daily ethical indifference in another way, apart from unloading the accumulated supplies of moral sentiments. Their long-term effect is that 'the developed part of the world surrounds itself with a sanitary belt of uncommitment, erects a global Berlin Wall; all information coming from "out there" are pictures of war, murders, drugs, looting, contagious diseases, refugees and hunger; that is, of something threatening to us.' Only rarely, and invariably in a hushed tone, and in no connection with the scenes of civil wars and massacres, we hear of the murderous weapons used for that purpose. Less often yet, if at all, are we reminded of what we know but prefer not to be told about: that all those weapons used to make the far-away homelands into killing fields have been supplied by our own arms factories, jealous of their order-books and proud of their productivity and global competitiveness – that lifeblood of our own cherished prosperity. A synthetic image of the *self-inflicted* brutality sediments in public consciousness – an image of 'mean streets', 'no-go areas' writ large, a magnified rendition of a gangland, an alien, subhuman world beyond ethics and beyond salvation. Attempts to save that world from the worst consequences of its own brutality may bring only momentary effects and are bound in the long run to fail; all the lifelines thrown may be easily retwisted into more nooses.

There is another important role played by the association of the 'far-away locals' with murder, epidemic and looting. Given their monstrosity, one cannot but thank God for making them what they are – the *far-away* locals, and pray that they stay that way.

The wish of the hungry to go where food is plentiful is what one would naturally expect from rational human beings; letting them act on their wishes is also what conscience would suggest is the right, moral thing to do. It is because of its undeniable rationality and ethical correctness that the rational and ethically conscious world feels so crestfallen in the face of the prospect of the mass migration of the poor and hungry; it is so difficult, without feeling guilty, to deny the poor and hungry their right to go where food is more plentiful; and it is virtually impossible to advance convincing rational arguments proving that their migration would be, for them, an unreasonable decision to take. The challenge is truly awesome: one needs to deny the others the self-same right to freedom of movement which one eulogizes as the topmost achievement of the globalizing world and the warrant of its growing prosperity . . .

The pictures of inhumanity which rules the lands where prospective migrants reside therefore comes in handy. They strengthen the resolve which lacks the rational and ethical arguments to support it. They help to keep the locals local, while allowing the globals to travel with a clear conscience.

4

Tourists and Vagabonds

Nowadays we are all on the move.

Many of us change places – moving homes or travelling to and from places which are not our homes. Some of us do not need to go out to travel: we can dash or scurry or flit through the Web, netting and mixing on the computer screen messages born in opposite corners of the globe. But most of us are on the move even if physically, bodily, we stay put. When, as is our habit, we are glued to our chairs and zap the cable or satellite channels on and off the TV screen – jumping in and out of foreign spaces with a speed much beyond the capacity of supersonic jets and cosmic rockets, but nowhere staying long enough to be more than visitors, to feel *chez soi*.

In the world we inhabit, distance does not seem to matter much. Sometimes it seems that it exists solely in order to be cancelled; as if space was but a constant invitation to slight it, refute and deny. Space stopped being an obstacle – one needs just a split second to conquer it.

There are no 'natural borders' any more, neither are there obvious places to occupy. Wherever we happen to be at the moment, we cannot help knowing that we could be elsewhere, so there is less and less reason to stay anywhere in particular (and thus we feel often an overwhelming urge to find – to compose – such a reason). Pascal's witty adage has turned out to be a prophecy come true: we indeed live in a strange circle whose centre is everywhere, and circumference nowhere (or, who knows, perhaps the other way round?).

And so spiritually at least we are all travellers. Or, as Michael Benedikt puts it, 'the very significance of geographical location at all scales begins to be questioned. We become nomads – who are always in touch.'[1] But we are on the move also in another, deeper sense, whether or not we take to the roads or leap through the channels, and whether we like doing it or detest it.

The idea of the 'state of rest', of immobility, makes sense only in a world that stays still or could be taken for such; in a place with solid walls, fixed roads and signposts steady enough to have time to rust. One cannot 'stay put' in moving sands. Neither can one stay put in this late-modern or postmodern world of ours – a world with reference points set on wheels and known for their vexing habit of vanishing from view before the instruction they offer has been read out in full, pondered and acted upon. Professor Ricardo Petrella of the Catholic University of Louvain recently summed it up very well: 'Globalization drags economies toward the production of the ephemeral, the volatile (through a massive and universal reduction of the life-span of products and services) and of the precarious (temporary, flexible and part-time jobs).'[2]

In order to elbow their way through the dense and dark, straggly, 'deregulated' thicket of global competitiveness and into the limelight of public attention – goods, services and signals must arouse desire, and in order to do so they must seduce their prospective consumers and out-seduce their competitors. But once they have done it they must make room, and quickly, for other objects of desire, lest the global chase of profit and ever greater profit (rebaptized as 'economic growth') shall grind to a halt. Today's industry is geared increasingly to the production of attractions and temptations. And it is in the nature of attractions that they tempt and seduce only as long as they beckon from that far-away which we call the future, while temptation cannot survive for long the surrender of the tempted – just as desire never survives its satisfaction.

For this chase after new desires, rather than after their satisfaction, there is no obvious finishing line. The very notion of the 'limit' must need temporal/spatial dimensions. The effect of 'taking the waiting out of wanting' is taking the wanting out of waiting. Once all delay can in principle be flattened into instantaneity, so that an infinite multitude of time-events can be packed into the time-span of human life, and once all distance seems fit to be compressed into co-presence so that no space-scale is in principle too big for the explorer of new sensations – what possible meaning could the idea of the 'limit' carry? And without sense, without a meaningful meaning, there is no way for the magic wheel of temptation and desire ever to run out of momentum. The consequences, for both the high and the lowly, are enormous – as cogently expressed by Jeremy Seabrook:

> Poverty cannot be 'cured', for it is not a symptom of the disease of capitalism. Quite the reverse: it is evidence of its robust good health, its spur to even greater accumulation and effort . . . Even the very richest in the world complain above all about all the things they must forego . . . Even the most privileged are compelled to bear within themselves the urgency for striving to acquire . . .[3]

Being a consumer in a consumer society

Our society is a consumer society.

When we speak of a consumer society, we have in mind something more than the trivial observation that all members of that society consume; all human beings, and, moreover, all living creatures, have been 'consuming' since time immemorial. What we do have in mind is that ours is a 'consumer society' in a similarly profound and fundamental sense in which the society of our predecessors, modern society in its foundation-laying, industrial phase, used to be a 'producers' society'. That older type of modern society engaged its members primarily as producers and soldiers; the way in which that society shaped its members, the 'norm' which it held up before their eyes and prompted them to observe, was dictated by the duty to play those two roles. The norm which that society held up to its members was the ability and the willingness to play them. But in its present late-modern (Giddens), second-modern (Beck), surmodern (Balandier) or postmodern stage, modern society has little need for mass industrial labour and conscript armies; instead, it needs to engage its members in their capacity as consumers. The way present-day society shapes its members is dictated first and foremost by the duty to play the role of the consumer. The norm our society holds up to its members is that of the ability and willingness to play it.

Of course, the difference between living in our society and living in its immediate predecessor is not as radical as abandoning one role and picking up another instead. In neither of its two stages could modern society do without its members producing things to be consumed – and members of both societies do, of course, consume. The difference between the two stages of modernity is one of emphasis and priorities 'only' – but that shift of emphasis does make an enormous difference to virtually every aspect of society, culture and individual life.

The differences are so deep and multiform that they fully justify speaking of our society as of a society of a separate and distinct kind – a consumer society. The consumer of a consumer society is a sharply different creature from consumers in any other societies thus far. If the philosophers, poets and moral preachers among our ancestors pondered the question whether one works in order to live or lives in order to work, the dilemma one hears mulled over most often nowadays is whether one needs to consume in order to live or whether one lives so that one can consume. That is, if we are still able, and feel the need to, tell apart the living from the consuming.

Ideally, all acquired habits should lie on the shoulders of that new type of consumer just like the ethically inspired vocational and acquisitive passions were hoped to lie, as Max Weber repeated after Baxter, on the shoulders of the Protestant saint: 'like a light cloak, ready to be thrown aside at any moment.'[4] And the habits are, indeed, continually, daily, and at the first opportunity thrown aside, never given the chance to firm up into the iron bars of a cage (except for one meta-habit, the 'habit of changing habits'). Ideally, nothing should be embraced by a consumer firmly, nothing should command a commitment till death do us part, no needs should be seen as fully satisfied, no desires considered ultimate. There ought to be a proviso 'until further notice' attached to any oath of loyalty and any commitment. It is but the volatility, the in-built temporality of all engagements, that truly counts; it counts more than the commitment itself, which is anyway not allowed to outlast the time necessary for consuming the object of desire (or, rather, the time sufficient for the desirability of that object to wane).

That all consumption takes time is in fact the bane of consumer society – and a major worry for the merchandisers of consumer goods. There is a natural resonance between the spectacular career of the 'now', brought about by time-compressing technology, and the logic of consumer-oriented economy. As far as the latter goes, the consumer's satisfaction ought to be *instant*: and this in a double sense. Obviously, consumed goods should satisfy immediately, requiring no learning of skills and no lengthy groundwork; but the satisfaction should also end – 'in no time', that is in the moment the time needed for their consumption is up. And that time ought to be reduced to the bare minimum.

The needed time-reduction is best achieved if consumers cannot hold their attention or focus their desire on any object for long; if they are impatient, impetuous and restive, and above all easily excitable and equally easily losing interest. The culture of consumer society is mostly about forgetting, not learning. Indeed, when the waiting is taken out of wanting and the wanting out of waiting, the consumption capacity of consumers may be stretched far beyond the limits set by any natural or acquired needs; also, the physical endurability of the objects of desire is no longer required. The traditional relationship between needs and their satisfaction is reversed: the promise and hope of satisfaction precedes the need promised to be satisfied and will be always more intense and alluring than the extant needs.

As a matter of fact, the promise is all the more attractive the less familiar is the need in question; there is a lot of fun in living through an experience one did not know existed, and a good consumer is a fun-loving adventurer. For good consumers it is not the satisfaction of the needs one is tormented by, but the torments of desires never yet sensed or suspected that makes the promise so tempting.

The kind of consumer gestated and incubated inside the society of consumers has been most poignantly described by John Carroll, taking his cue from Nietzsche's caustic yet prophetic caricature of the 'last man' (see Carroll's forthcoming book: *Ego and Soul: a Sociology of the Modern West in the Search of Meaning*):

> The ethos of this society proclaims: If you feel bad, eat! . . . The consumerist reflex is melancholic, supposing that malaise takes the form of feeling empty, cold, flat – in need of filling up warm, rich, vital things. Of course it need not be food, as in what made The Beatles 'feel happy inside'. Gorging is the path to salvation – consume and feel good! . . .
>
> There is equally the restlessness, the mania for constant change, movement, difference – to sit still is to die . . . Consumerism is thus the social analogue to the psychopathology of depression, with its twin clashing symptoms of enervation and inability to sleep.

For the consumers in the society of consumers, being on the move – searching, looking for, not-finding-it or more exactly not-finding-it-yet is not a malaise, but the promise of bliss; perhaps it is the bliss itself. Theirs is the kind of travelling hopefully which makes arriving into a curse. (Maurice Blanchot noted that the answer is the bad luck of the question; we may say that the satisfaction is the bad luck of the desire.) Not so much the greed to acquire and possess, not the gathering of wealth in its material, tangible sense, as the excitement of a new and unprecedented sensation is the name of the consumer game. Consumers are first and foremost gatherers of *sensations*; they are collectors of *things* only in a secondary and derivative sense.

Mark C. Taylor and Esa Saarinen put it in a nutshell: 'desire does not desire satisfaction. To the contrary, desire desires desire.'[5] The desire of an ideal consumer at any rate. The prospect of the desire fading off and dissipating, the prospect of being left with nothing in sight to resurrect it or with a world with nothing in it to be desired, must be the most sinister of the ideal consumer's horrors (and of the merchandisers of consumer goods' nightmares, of course).

To increase their capacity for consumption, consumers must never be allowed to rest. They need to be kept forever awake and on the alert, constantly exposed to new temptations and so remain in a state of a never wilting excitation – and also, indeed, a state of perpetual suspicion and steady disaffection. The baits commanding them to shift attention need to confirm the suspicion while promising the way out of disaffection: 'You reckon'd you seen it all? You ain't seen nothin' yet!'

It is often said that the consumer market seduces its customers. But in order to do so it needs customers who *want* to be seduced (just as to command his labourers, the factory boss needed a crew with the habits of discipline and command-following firmly entrenched). In a properly working consumer society consumers seek actively to be seduced. Their grand-fathers, the producers, lived from one turn of the conveyor belt to an identical next. They themselves, for a change, live from attraction to attraction, from temptation to temptation, from sniffing out one tidbit to searching for another, from swallowing one bait to fishing around for another – each attraction, temptation, tidbit and bait being new, different and more attention-catching than its predecessor.

To act like this is for fully fledged, mature consumers a compulsion, a must; yet that 'must', that internalized pressure, that impossibility of living one's life in any other way, reveals itself to them in the disguise of a free exercise of will. The market might already have selected them as consumers and so taken away their freedom to ignore its blandishments; but on every successive visit to a market-place consumers have every reason to feel that it is they – perhaps even they alone – who are in command. They are the judges, the critics and the choosers. They can, after all, refuse their allegiance to any one of the infinite choices on display. Except the choice of choosing between them, that is – but that choice does not appear to be a choice.

It is this combination of the consumers, constantly greedy for new attractions and fast bored with attractions already had, and of the world transformed in all its dimensions – economic, political, or personal – after the pattern of the consumer market and, like the market, ready to oblige and change its attractions with ever accelerating speed, that wipes out all fixed signposts – steel, concrete, or plotted of authority only – from the individual maps of the world and from the designs of life itineraries. Indeed, travelling hopefully is in the life of the consumer much more pleasurable than to arrive. Arrival has that musty smell of the end of the road, that bitter taste of monotony and stagnation which would put paid to everything which the consumer – the ideal consumer – lives by and for and views as the sense of living. To enjoy the best that this world has to offer, you may do all sorts of things except one: to declare, after Goethe's Faust: 'O moment, you are beautiful, last forever!'

The consumer is a person on the move and bound to remain so.

Divided we move

One thing which even the most seasoned and discerning masters of the art of choice do not and cannot choose, is the society to be born into – and so we are all in travel, whether we like it or not. We have not been asked about our feelings anyway.

Thrown into a vast open sea with no navigation charts and all the marker buoys sunk and barely visible, we have only two choices left: we may rejoice in the breath-taking vistas of new discoveries – or we may tremble out of fear of drowning. One option not really realistic is to claim sanctuary in a safe harbour; one could bet that what seems to be a tranquil haven today will be soon modernized, and a theme park, amusement promenade or crowded marina will replace the sedate boat sheds. The third option not thus being available, which of the two other options will be chosen or become the lot of the sailor depends in no small measure on the ship's quality and the navigating skills of the sailors. The stronger the ship, the less reason to fear the tides and sea storms. Not all ships are seaworthy, however. And so the larger the expanse of free sailing, the more the sailors' fate tends to be polarized and the deeper the chasm between the poles. A pleasurable adventure for the well-equipped yacht may prove a dangerous trap for a tattered dinghy. In the last account, the difference between the two is that between life and death.

Everybody may be *cast* into the mode of the consumer; everybody may *wish* to be a consumer and indulge in the opportunities which that mode of life holds. But not everybody *can* be a consumer. To desire is not enough; to make the desire truly desirable, and so to draw the pleasure from the desire, one must have a reasonable hope of getting closer to the desired object. This hope, reasonably entertained by some, is futile for many others. All of us are doomed to the life of choices, but not all of us have the means to be choosers.

Like all other known societies, the postmodern, consumer society is a stratified one. But it is possible to tell one kind of society from another by the dimensions along which it stratifies its members. The dimension along which those 'high up' and 'low down' are plotted in a society of consumers, is their *degree of mobility* – their freedom to choose where to be.

One difference between those 'high up' and those 'low down' is that the first may leave the second behind – but not vice versa. Contemporary cities are sites of an 'apartheid à rebours': those who can afford it, abandon the filth and squalor of the regions that those who cannot afford the move are stuck to. In Washington D.C. they have already done it – in Chicago, Cleveland and Baltimore they are close to having done it. In Washington no discrimination is practised on the house market. And yet there is an invisible border stretching along 16th Street in the west and the Potomac river in the north-west, which those left behind are wise never to cross. Most of the adolescents left behind the invisible yet all-too-tangible border never saw downtown Washington with all its splendours, ostentatious elegance and refined pleasures. In their life, that downtown does not exist. There is no talking over the border. The life experiences are so sharply different that it is not clear what the residents of the two sides could talk to each other about were they to meet and stop to converse. As Ludwig Wittgenstein remarked, 'If lions could talk, we would not understand them.'

And another difference. Those 'high up' are satisfied that they travel through life by their heart's desire and pick and choose their destinations according to the joys they offer. Those 'low down' happen time and again to be thrown out from the site they would rather stay in. (In 1975 there were 2 million forced emigrants – refugees – under the care of the High

Commission set by the UN for that purpose. In 1995 there were 27 million of them.) If they do not move, it is often the site that is pulled from under their feet, so it feels like being on the move anyway. If they take to the roads, then their destination, more often than not, is of somebody else's choice; it is seldom enjoyable, and its enjoyability is not what it has been chosen for. They might occupy a highly unprepossessing site which they would gladly leave behind – but they have nowhere else to go, since nowhere else they are likely to be welcomed and allowed to put up a tent.

Progressively, entry visas are phased out all over the globe. But not passport control. The latter is still needed – perhaps more than ever before – to sort out the confusion which the abolition of the visas might have created: to set apart those for whose convenience and whose ease of travel the visas have been abolished, from those who should have stayed put – not meant to travel in the first place. The present-day combination of the annulment of entry visas and the reinforcement of immigration controls has profound symbolic significance. It could be taken as the metaphor for the new, emergent, stratification. It lays bare the fact that it is now the 'access to global mobility' which has been raised to the topmost rank among the stratifying factors. It also reveals the global dimension of all privilege and deprivation, however local. Some of us enjoy the new freedom of movement *sans papiers*. Some others are not allowed to stay put for the same reason.

All people may now be wanderers, in fact or in premonition – but there is an abyss hard to bridge between experiences likely to emerge, respectively, at the top and at the bottom of the freedom scale. The fashionable term 'nomads', applied indiscriminately to all contemporaries of the postmodern era, is grossly misleading, as it glosses over the profound differences which separate the two types of experience and render all similarity between them formal and superficial.

As a matter of fact, the worlds sedimented on the two poles, at the top and at the bottom of the emergent hierarchy of mobility, differ sharply; they also become increasingly incommunicado to each other. For the first world, the world of the globally mobile, the space has lost its constraining quality and is easily traversed in both its 'real' and 'virtual' renditions. For the second world, the world of the 'locally tied', of those barred from moving and thus bound to bear passively whatever change may be visited on the locality they are tied to, the real space is fast closing up. This is a kind of deprivation which is made yet more painful by the obtrusive media display of the space conquest and of the '*virtual* accessibility' of distances that stay stubbornly unreachable in non-virtual reality.

The shrinking of space abolishes the flow of time. The inhabitants of the first world live in a perpetual present, going through a succession of episodes hygienically insulated from their past as well as their future. These people are constantly busy and perpetually 'short of time', since each moment of time is non-extensive – an experience identical with that of time 'full to the brim'. People marooned in the opposite world are crushed under the burden of abundant, redundant and useless time they have nothing to fill with. In their time 'nothing ever happens'. They do not 'control' time – but neither are they controlled by it, unlike their clocking-in, clocking-out ancestors, subject to the faceless rhythm of factory time. They can only kill time, as they are slowly killed by it.

Residents of the first world live in *time*; space does not matter for them, since spanning every distance is instantaneous. It is this experience which Jean Baudrillard encapsulated in his image of 'hyperreality', where the virtual and the real are no longer separable, since both share or miss in the same measure that 'objectivity', 'externality' and 'punishing power' which Emile Durkheim listed as the symptoms of all reality. Residents of the second world, on the contrary, live in *space*: heavy, resilient, untouchable, which ties down time and keeps it beyond the residents' control. Their time is void; in their time, 'nothing ever happens'. Only the virtual, TV time has a structure, a 'timetable' – the rest of time is monotonously ticking away; it comes and goes, making no demands and apparently leaving no trace. Its sediments appear all of a sudden, unannounced and uninvited. Immaterial and light-weight, ephemeral, with nothing to fill it with sense and so give it gravity, time has no power over that all-too-real space to which the residents of the second world are confined.

For the inhabitants of the first world – the increasingly cosmopolitan, extraterritorial world of global businessmen, global culture managers or global academics, state borders are levelled down, as they are dismantled for the world's commodities, capital and finances. For the inhabitant of the second world, the walls built of immigration controls, of residence laws and of 'clean streets' and 'zero tolerance' policies, grow taller; the moats separating them from the sites of their desire and of dreamed-of redemption grow deeper, while all bridges, at the first attempt to cross them, prove to be drawbridges. The first travel at will, get much fun from their travel (particularly if travelling first class or using private aircraft), are cajoled or bribed to travel and welcomed with smiles and open arms when they do. The second travel surreptitiously, often illegally, some-times paying more for the crowded steerage of a stinking unseaworthy boat than others pay for business-class gilded luxuries – and are frowned upon, and, if unlucky, arrested and promptly deported, when they arrive.

Moving through the world vs. the world moving by

The cultural/psychological consequences of polarization are enormous.

Larry Elliott in *The Guardian* of 10 November 1997 quotes Diane Coyle, the author of *The Weightless World*, who expatiates on the pleasures which the new brave electronic computerized flexible world of high speed and mobility offers her personally: 'For people like me, a well educated and well paid economist and journalist with a degree of entrepreneurial spirit, the new flexibility of the UK labour market has provided wonderful opportunities.' But a few paragraphs later the same author admits that for 'people without suitable qualifications, adequate family resources or enough savings, increased flexibility boils down to being exploited more thoroughly by employers . . .' Coyle asks that the recent warning of Lester Thurow and Robert Reich about the growing dangers of social chasm growing in the USA between 'a rich elite holed up in guarded compounds' and 'a workless impoverished majority' should not be treated lightly by all those basking in the sunshine of the new British labour flexibility . . .

Agnes Heller recalls meeting, on one of her long-distance flights, a middle-aged woman, an employee of an international trade firm, who spoke five languages and owned three apartments in three different places.

> She constantly migrates, and among many places, and always to and fro. She does it alone, not as a member of community, although many people act like her . . . The kind of culture she participates in is not a culture of a certain place; it is the culture of a time. It is a culture of the *absolute present*.
>
> Let's accompany her on her constant trips from Singapore to Hong Kong, London, Stockholm, New Hampshire, Tokyo, Prague and so on. She stays in the same Hilton hotel, eats the same tuna sandwich for lunch, or, if she wishes, eats Chinese food in Paris and French food in Hong Kong. She uses the same type of fax, and telephones, and computers, watches the same films, and discusses the same kind of problems with the same kind of people.

Agnes Heller, herself like many of us an academic globetrotter, finds it easy to empathize with her anonymous companion's experience. She adds, *pro domo sua*: 'Even foreign universities are not foreign. After one delivers a lecture, one can expect the same questions in Singapore, Tokyo, Paris or Manchester. They are not foreign places, nor are they homes.' Agnes Heller's companion has no home – but neither does she feel homeless. Wherever she is at the moment, she feels at ease. 'For example, she knows where the electric switch is; she knows the menu in advance; she reads the gestures and the allusions; she understands others without further explanation.'[6]

Jeremy Seabrook remembers another woman, Michelle, from a neighbouring council estate:

> At fifteen her hair was one day red, the next blonde, then jet-black, then teased into Afro kinks and after that rat-tails, then plaited, and then cropped so that it glistened close to the skull . . . Her lips were scarlet, then purple, then black. Her face was ghost-white and then peach-coloured, then bronze as if it were cast in metal. Pursued by dreams of flight, she left home at sixteen to be with her boyfriend, who was twenty-six . . .
>
> At eighteen she returned to her mother, with two children . . . She sat in the bedroom which she had fled three years earlier; the faded photos of yesterday's pop stars still stared down from the walls. She said she felt a hundred years old. She'd tried all that life could offer. Nothing else was left.[7]

Heller's fellow-passenger lives in an imaginary home she does not need and thus does not mind being imaginary. Seabrook's acquaintance performs imaginary flights from the home she resents for being stultifyingly real. Virtuality of space serves both, but to each offers different services with sharply different results. To Heller's travel companion, it helps to dissolve whatever constraints a real home may impose – to dematerialize space without exposing herself to the discomforts and the anxieties of homelessness. To Seabrook's neighbour, it brings into relief the awesome and abhorrent power of a home turned into prison – it decomposes time. The first experience is lived through as postmodern freedom. The second may feel rather uncannily like the postmodern version of slavery.

The first experience is, paradigmatically, that of the *tourist* (and it does not matter whether the purpose of the trip is business or pleasure). Tourists become wanderers and put the bitter-sweet dreams of homesickness above the comforts of home – because they want to; either because they consider it the most reasonable life-strategy 'under the circumstances', or because they have been seduced by the true or imaginary pleasures of a sensations-gatherer's life.

Not all wanderers, however, are on the move because they prefer being on the move to staying put and because they want to go where they are going. Many would perhaps go elsewhere or refuse to embark on a life of wandering altogether – were they asked, but they had not been asked in the first place. If they are on the move, it is because 'staying at home' in a world made to the measure of the tourist feels like humiliation and a drudgery and in the long run does not seem a feasible proposition anyway. They are on the move because they have been pushed from behind – having first been spiritually uprooted from the place that holds no promise, by a force of seduction or propulsion too powerful, and often too mysterious, to resist. They see their plight as anything except the manifestation of freedom. These are the *vagabonds*; dark vagrant moons reflecting the shine of bright tourist suns and following placidly the planets' orbit; the mutants of postmodern evolution, the monster rejects of the brave new species. The vagabonds are the waste of the world which has dedicated itself to tourist services.

The tourists stay or move at their hearts' desire. They abandon a site when new untried opportunities beckon elsewhere. The vagabonds know that they won't stay in a place for long, however strongly they wish to, since nowhere they stop are they likely to be welcome. The tourists move because they find the world within their (global) reach irresistibly *attractive* – the vagabonds move because they find the world within their (local) reach unbearably *inhospitable*. The tourists travel because *they want to*; the vagabonds because *they have no other bearable choice*. The vagabonds are, one may say, involuntary tourists; but the notion of 'involuntary tourist' is a contradiction in terms. However much the tourist's strategy may be a necessity in a world marked by shifting walls and mobile roads, freedom of choice is the tourist's flesh and blood. Take it away, and the attraction, the poetry and, indeed, the liveability of the tourist's life are all but gone.

What is acclaimed today as 'globalization' is geared to the tourists' dreams and desires. Its second effect – a *side*-effect, but an unavoidable one – is the transformation of many others into vagabonds. Vagabonds are travellers refused the right to turn into tourists. They are allowed neither to stay put (there is no site guaranteeing permanence, the end to undesirable mobility) nor search for a better place to be.

Once emancipated from space, capital no longer needs itinerant labour (while its most emancipated, most advanced high-tech avant-garde needs hardly *any* labour, mobile or immobile). And so the pressure to pull down the last remaining barriers to the free movement of money and money-making commodities and information goes hand in hand with the pressure to dig new moats and erect new walls (variously called 'immigration' or 'nationality' laws) barring the movement of those who are uprooted, spiritually or bodily, as a result.[8] *Green light for the tourists, red light for the vagabonds.* Enforced localization guards the natural selectivity of the globalizing effects. The widely noted, increasingly worrying polarization of the world and its population is not an external, alien, disturbing, 'spoke in the wheel' interference with the process of globalization; it is its effect.

There are no tourists without the vagabonds, and the tourists cannot be let free without tying down the vagabonds . . .

For better or worse – united

The vagabond is the *alter ego* of the tourist. He is also the tourist's most ardent admirer – all the more so for the fact of having no inkling of the real, but not much talked about, inconveniences of the tourist's life. Ask the vagabonds what sort of life they would wish to have, given the chance of free choice – and you will get a pretty accurate description of the tourist's bliss 'as seen on TV'. Vagabonds have no other images of the good life – no alternative utopia, no political agenda of their own. The sole thing they want is to be allowed to be tourists – like the rest of us . . . In a restless world, tourism is the only acceptable, human form of restlessness.

The tourist and the vagabond are both consumers, and late-modern or postmodern consumers are sensation-seekers and collectors of experiences; their relationship to the world is primarily *aesthetic*: they perceive the world as a food for sensibility – a matrix of possible experiences (in the sense of *Erlebnisse*, a state one lives through, not *Erfahrungen*, occurrences that happen to one – the seminal distinction made in German, but sorely missing in English); and they map it according to the experiences occasioned. Both are touched – attracted or repelled – by the promised sensations. They both 'savour' the world, as seasoned museum-goers savour their *tête-à-tête* with a work of art. This attitude-to-the-world unites them, makes them like each other. This is the kind of similarity which enables the vagabonds to empathize with tourists, with their images of tourists at any rate – and to desire a share in their life-style; but a similarity which the tourists try hard to forget – though much to their dismay cannot fully and truly repress.

As Jeremy Seabrook reminds his readers,[9] the secret of present-day society lies in 'the development of an artificially created and subjective sense of insufficiency' – since 'nothing could be more menacing' to its foundational principles 'than that the people should declare themselves satisfied with what they have'. What people do have is thus played down, denigrated, dwarfed by the obtrusive and all-too-visible displays of extravagant adventures by the better-off: 'The rich become objects of universal adoration.'

The rich who were put on display as personal heroes for universal adoration and the patterns of universal emulation used once to be the 'self-made men', whose lives epitomized the benign effects of the work ethic and of reason strictly and doggedly adhered to. This is no longer the case. The object of adoration is now wealth itself – wealth as the warrant for a most fanciful and prodigal life-style. It is *what one can do* that matters, not *what is to be done* or *what has been done*. Universally adored in the persons of the rich is their wondrous ability to pick and choose the contents of their lives, places to live in now and then, partners to share those places with – and to change all of them at will and without effort; the fact that they seem never to reach points of no return, that there is no visible end to their reincarnations, that their future looks forever richer in content and more enticing than their past; and, last but not least, that the only thing which seems to matter to them is the range of prospects their wealth seems to throw open. These people seem, indeed, to be guided by the aesthetics of consumption; it is the display of extravagant, even frivolous aesthetic taste, not the obedience to work ethic or dry, abstemious precept of reason, the connoisseurship, not a mere financial success, that lie at the heart of their perceived greatness and founds their right to universal admiration.

'The poor do not inhabit a separate culture from the rich', Seabrook points out, 'they must live in the same world that has been contrived for the benefit of those with money. And their poverty is aggravated by economic growth, just as it is intensified by recession and non-growth.' Indeed, recession spells more poverty and fewer resources; but the growth ushers in a still more frantic display of consumer wonders and thus augurs a deeper gap yet between the desirable and the realistic.

Both the tourist and the vagabond have been made into consumers, but the vagabond is a _flawed_ consumer. The vagabonds are not really able to afford the kind of sophisticated choices in which the consumers are expected to excel; their potential for consumption is as limited as their resources. This fault makes their position in society precarious. They breach the norm and sap the order. They spoil the fun simply by being around, they do not lubricate the wheels of the consumer society, they add nothing to the prosperity of the economy turned into a tourist industry. They are useless, in the sole sense of 'use' one can think of in a society of consumers or society of tourists. And because they are useless, they are also unwanted. Being unwanted, they are natural objects for stigmatizing and scapegoating. But their crime is nothing other than to wish to be like the tourists – while lacking the means to act on their wishes the way the tourists do.

But if the tourists view them as unsavoury, disreputable and offensive, and resent their unsolicited company, it is for deeper reasons than the much publicized 'public costs' of keeping the vagabonds alive. The tourists have a horror of the vagabonds for much the same reason that the vagabonds look up to the tourists as their gurus and idols: in the society of travellers, in the travelling society, tourism and vagrancy are two faces of the same coin. The vagabond, let us repeat, is the _alter ego_ of the tourist. The line which divides them is tenuous and not always clearly drawn. One can easily cross it without noticing . . . There is this abominable likeness which makes it so hard to decide at which point the portrait becomes a caricature and the proper and healthy specimen of the species turns into a mutant and a monster.

There are among the tourists some 'regular goers', always on the go and always confident that they go in the right direction and that the going is the right thing to do; these happy tourists are seldom worried by the thought that their escapades may

descend into vagabondage. And there are some hopeless vagabonds, who long ago threw in the towel and abandoned all hope
of ever rising to the rank of tourists. But between these two
extremes there is a large part, arguably a substantial majority of
the society of consumers/travellers, who cannot be quite sure
where do they stand at the moment and even less can be sure
that their present standing will see the light of the next day.
There are so many banana skins on the road, and so many
sharp kerbs on which one can stumble. After all, most jobs are
temporary, shares may go down as well as up, skills keep being
devalued and superseded by new and improved skills, the assets
one is proud of and cherishes now become obsolete in no time,
exquisite neighbourhoods become shoddy and vulgar, partner-
ships are formed merely until further notice, values worth
pursuing and ends worth investing come and go . . . Just as no
life insurance protects the policy owner from death, none of the
insurance policies of the tourist's life-style protects against
slipping into vagabondage.

And so the vagabond is the tourist's nightmare; the tourist's
'inner demon' which needs to be exorcized, and daily. The
sight of the vagabond makes the tourist tremble – not because
of *what the vagabond is* but becaue of *what the tourist may become.*
While sweeping the vagabond under the carpet – banning the
beggar and the homeless from the street, confining him to a far-
away, 'no-go' ghetto, demanding his exile or incarceration – the
tourist desperately, though in the last account vainly, seeks the
deportation of his own fears. A world without vagabonds will
be a world in which Gregor Samsa will never undergo the
metamorphosis into an insect, and the tourists will never wake
up vagabonds. *A world without vagabonds is the utopia of the
society of tourists.* Much of the politics in the society of tourists –
like the obsession with 'law and order', the criminalization of
poverty, recurrent spongers-bashing etc. – can be explained as
an ongoing, stubborn effort to lift social reality, against all odds,
to the level of that utopia.

The snag is, though, that the life of tourists would not be half as enjoyable as it is, were there no vagabonds around to show what the alternative to that life, the sole alternative which the society of travellers renders realistic, would be like. Tourist life is not a bed of roses, and the roses most likely to be found there grow on unpleasantly thorny stems. There are many hardships one needs to suffer for the sake of tourist's freedoms: the impossibility of slowing down, uncertainty wrapping every choice, risks attached to every decision being the most prominent, but not the only ones among them. Besides, the joy of choosing tends to lose much of its allure when choose you *must*, and adventure is stripped of a good deal of its attraction once one's whole life becomes a string of adventures. And so there are quite a few things the tourist could complain about. The temptation to seek another, non-tourist way to happiness is never far away. It can be never extinguished, but can only be pushed aside, and then not for long. What makes the tourist life endurable, turns its hardship into minor irritants and allows the temptation to change to be kept on a back shelf, is the self-same sight of the vagabond that makes the tourists shudder.

And so, paradoxically, the tourist's life is all the more bearable, even enjoyable, for being haunted with a uniformly nightmarish alternative of the vagabond's existence. In an equally paradoxical sense, the tourists have vested interest in rendering that alternative as dreadful and execrable as possible. The less appetizing is the vagabond's fate, the more savoury are the tourist's peregrinations. The worse is the plight of the vagabonds, the better it feels to be a tourist. Were there no vagabonds, the tourists would need to invent them . . . The world of travellers needs them both, and together – bound to each other in a Gordian knot no one seems to know how to untie and no one seems to have (or to seek) a sword to cut.

And so we go on moving – the tourists and the vagabonds, half-tourists/half-vagabonds that most of us are in this society of consumers/travellers of ours. Our plights are more tightly intertwined than the touristic preoccupations, as long as they last, allow to admit.

But the two fates and life-experiences that shared plight gestates prompt two sharply different perceptions of the world, of the world's ills, and of the ways to repair the ills – different, yet alike in their failings, in their tendency to gloss over the network of mutual dependency which underlies each of them as well as their opposition.

On the one hand, there is an ideology taking shape in the accounts of the spokesmen for the globals, among whom Jonathan Friedman lists 'intellectuals close to the media; the media intelligentsia itself; in a certain sense, all those who can afford a cosmopolitan identity';[10] or, rather, the tacit assumptions which make that ideology credible simply by the refusal to question it: a sort of assumptions which Pierre Bourdieu described recently as *doxa* – 'an evidence not debated and undebatable'.[11]

On the other hand, there are the actions of the locals and forcefully localized, or, more exactly, those who try, with growing success, to take into their political sails the winds of wrath blowing from the *glebae adscripti* quarters. The resulting clash does nothing to rectify the schism and everything to deepen it still further, directing political imagination away from the true cause of the plight both sides bewail – though each for ostensibly opposite reasons.

Friedman pokes fun at the language of cosmopolitan chatter – all these *en vogue* terms of 'in-betweenness', 'dis-juncture', 'trans-cendence' etc. which allegedly do more than to articulate the experience of those who have already cut their anchors free, those 'already emancipated' – which would also articulate the experience of the not-yet-emancipated, were it not for the latter's ugly and off-putting tendency to 'boundedness' and 'essentialization'. This language presents privilege, complete with its specific insecurities, as shared 'human nature' or the 'future of us all'. However, Friedman asks, for whom

is such cultural transmigration a reality? In the work of the post-
colonial border-crossers, it is always the poet, the artist, the
intellectual, who sustains this displacement and objectifies it in
the printed word. But who reads the poetry, and what are the
other kinds of identification occurring in the lower reaches of
social reality? . . . Briefly, hybrids and hybridization theorists are
products of a group that self-identifies and/or identifies the world
in such terms, not as a result of ethnographic understanding, but
as an act of self-definition . . . The global, culturally hybrid, elite
sphere is occupied by individuals who share a very different kind
of experience of the world, connected to international politics,
academia, the media and the arts.

The cultural hybridization of the globals may be a creative,
emancipating experience, but cultural disempowerment of the
locals seldom is; it is an understandable, yet unfortunate
inclination of the first to confuse the two and so to present their
own variety of 'false consciousness' as a proof of the mental
impairment of the second.

But for those second – the locals by fate rather than choice –
the deregulation, dissipation of communal networks and force-
ful individualization of destiny portend quite different plight
and suggest quite different strategies. To quote Friedman once
more:

The logics that develops in underclass neighbourhoods is likely
to be of a different nature from those that develop among the
highly educated world travellers of the culture industries . . . The
urban poor, ethnically mixed ghetto is an arena that does not
immediately cater to the construction of explicitly new hybrid
identities. In periods of global stability and/or expansion, the
problems of survival are more closely related to territory and to
creating secure life spaces. Class identity, local ghetto identity,
tend to prevail . . .

Two worlds, two perceptions of the world, two strategies.
And the paradox: this *postmodern* reality of the deregulated/

privatized/consumerist world, the globalizing/localizing world, finds only a pale, one-sided and grossly distorted reflection in the *postmodernist* narrative. The hybridization and defeat of essentialisms proclaimed by the postmodernist eulogy of the 'globalizing' world are far from conveying the complexity and sharp contradictions tearing that world apart. Postmodernism, one of many possible accounts of postmodern reality, merely articulates a caste-bound experience of the globals – the vociferous, highly audible and influential, yet relatively narrow category of exterritorials and globetrotters. It leaves unaccounted for and unarticulated other experiences, which are also an integral part of the postmodern scene.

Wojciech J. Burszta, the eminent Polish anthropologist, thus reflects on the results of this potentially disastrous breakdown in communication:

> Former peripheries clearly go their own way, making light of what the postmodernists tell about them. And they [the postmodernists – Z.B.] are rather helpless, when facing the realities of the militant Islam, the ugliness of Mexico City hovels or even the black squatting in a gutted South Bronx house. These are huge margins, and one does not know how to deal with them . . .
>
> Under the thin film of global symbols, labels and utilities a cauldron of the unknown seethes – in which we are not particularly interested and on which in fact we have little to say.[12]

'Peripheries' in the above quotation are best understood in a generic sense: as are all those infinitely numerous spaces which have been deeply affected by the 'global symbols, labels and utilities' – though not in the fashion anticipated by their globalist eulogists. 'Peripheries' in this sense spread all around the small, spiritually exterritorial yet physically heavily fortified, enclaves of the 'globalized' elite.

The paradox mentioned a moment ago leads to another: the age of 'time/space compression', uninhibited transfer of information and instantaneous communication – is also the age of an almost complete communication breakdown between the learned elites and the *populus*. The first ('the modernists without modernism', in Friedman's apt expression – that is, without a universalizing project) have nothing to say to the second; nothing that would reverberate in their minds as the echo of their own life experience and life prospects.

5

Global Law, Local Orders

In the United States, says Pierre Bourdieu, referring to the study of French sociologist Loïc Wacquant,

> the 'Charitable State', founded on the moralizing conception of poverty, tends to bifurcate into a Social State which assures minimal guarantees of security for the middle classes, and an increasingly repressive state counteracting the effects of violence which results from the increasingly precarious condition of the large mass of the population, notably the black.[1]

This is but one example – though admittedly a particularly blatant and spectacular one, like most American versions of wider, also global phenomena – of a much more general trend to limit the remnants of the original political initiative still held in the fast weakening hands of the nation-state to the issue of law and order; an issue which inevitably translates in practice as orderly – safe – existence for some, all the awesome and threatening force of the law for the others.

Bourdieu wrote the quoted article, delivered as a lecture in Freiburg in October 1996, as a sort of 'gut reaction' to a statement he read on the plane. The statement in question was made, matter-of-factly, almost perfunctorily, the way one speaks of obvious and banal truths, and without provoking any brow-raising among the audience or the readers, by Hans

Tietmeyer, the president of the German Federal Bank. 'Today's stake', said Tietmeyer, 'is to create conditions favourable to the confidence of investors.' Tietmeyer went on to spell out, again briefly and without much argument, in the way one speaks of things which are seen as self-evident to everyone the moment they are said, what such conditions would amount to. To make investors confident, to encourage them to invest, he said, would necessarily entail a tighter control of public expenditure, the lowering of the level of taxation, reforming the system of social protection and 'dismantling the rigidities of the labour market'.

The labour market is too rigid; it needs to be made flexible. That means more pliant and compliant, easy to knead and mould, to slice and roll, and putting up no resistance whatever is being done to it. In other words, labour is 'flexible' in as far as it becomes a kind of economic variable which investors may leave out of their account, certain that it will be their actions and their actions alone which will determine its conduct. To think of it, though, the idea of 'flexible labour' denies in practice what it asserts in theory. Or, rather, in order to implement what it postulates it must deprive its object of that agility and versatility which it exhorts it to acquire.

Like most front-line values, the idea of 'flexibility' hides its nature of social relation: the fact that it demands redistribution of power, and implies an intention to expropriate the power of resistance of those whose 'rigidity' is about to be overcome. Indeed, labour would cease to be 'rigid' only if it stopped being an unknown quantity in the investors' calculation. If it effectively lost the power to be truly 'flexible' – to refuse to conform to a pattern, to surprise, and all in all to put a limit on the investors' freedom of manoeuvre. 'Flexibility' only pretends to be a 'universal principle' of economic sanity, one that applies in equal measure to both the demand and the supply side of the labour market. The sameness of the term conceals its sharply different substance on each side of the divide.

Flexibility of the demand side means freedom to move

wherever greener pastures beckon, leaving the refuse and waste spattered around the last camp for the left-behind locals to clean up; above all, it means freedom to disregard all considerations except such as 'make economic sense'. What looks, however, like flexibility on the demand side, rebounds on all those cast on the supply side as hard, cruel, impregnable and unassailable fate: jobs come and go, they vanish as soon as they appeared, they are cut in pieces and withdrawn without notice while the rules of the hiring/firing game change without warning – and there is little the job-holders and job-seekers may do to stop the see-saw. And so to meet the standards of flexibility set for them by those who make and unmake the rules – to be 'flexible' in the eyes of the investors – the plight of the 'suppliers of labour' must be as rigid and *inflexible* as possible – indeed, the very contrary of 'flexible': their freedom to choose, to accept or refuse, let alone to impose their own rules on the game, must be cut to the bare bone.

The asymmetry of conditions expresses itself in the respective degrees of predictability. The side whose range of behavioural choices is wider introduces the element of uncertainty into the condition of the other side, which that side, facing a much narrower choice or no choice at all, cannot reciprocate. The *global* dimension of the investors' choices, when set against the strictly *local* limits of the 'labour supplier' choice, provides that asymmetry which in its turn underlies the domination of the first over the second. Mobility and its absence designate the new, late-modern or postmodern polarization of social conditions. The top of the new hierarchy is exterritorial; its lower ranges are marked by varying degrees of space constraints, while the bottom ones are, for all practical purposes, *glebae adscripti*.

Factories of immobility

Bourdieu points out that the State of California, celebrated by some European sociologists as the very paradise of liberty, dedicates to the building and the running costs of prisons a budget transcending by far the sum total of state funds allocated to all the institutions of higher education. Imprisonment is the ultimate and most radical form of spatial confinement. It also seems to be the main concern and focus of attention of the government by the political elite at the forefront of contemporary 'time/space compression'.

Spatial confinement, incarceration of varying degrees of stringency and harshness, has been at all times the prime method of dealing with the unassimilable, difficult-to-control, and otherwise trouble-prone sectors of the population. Slaves were confined to the slave quarters. So were lepers, madmen, and ethnic or religious aliens. If allowed to wander beyond the allotted quarters, they were obliged to wear the signs of their spatial assignment so that everybody was aware that they belonged to another space. Spatial separation leading to enforced confinement has been over the centuries almost a visceral, instinctual fashion of responding to all difference, and particularly such difference that could not be, or was not wished to be, accommodated within the web of habitual social intercourse. The deepest meaning of spatial separation was the banning or suspension of communication, and so the forcible perpetuation of estrangement.

Estrangement is the core function of spatial separation. Estrangement reduces, thins down and compresses the view of the other: individual qualities and circumstances which tend to be vividly brought within sight thanks to the accumulated experience of daily intercourse, seldom come into view when the intercourse is emaciated or prohibited altogether: typification takes then the place of personal familiarity, and legal categories meant to reduce the variance and to allow it to be disregarded render the uniqueness of persons and cases irrelevant.

As Nils Christie pointed out,[2] when personal familiarity prevails in daily life, concern with compensation for the harm done prevails over the demand for retribution and the punishment of the culprit. However angry we may be with the person responsible, we would not apply to the case the categories of penal law (we would not even think about the case in the terms of endemically impersonal categories of crime and punishment, to which paragraphs of law may be applied) 'because we know too much . . . In that totality of knowledge a legal category is much too narrow.' Now, however, we live among people we do not know and most of whom we are unlikely ever to know. It was natural to abstain from resorting to the cold letter of the law if the act which prompted our wrath was seen for what it was – not really like other acts 'of the same category'. 'But this is not necessarily true of the strange kid who just moved in across the street.' And so, says Christie, it is not entirely unexpected (even if not inevitable either), that the consistent trend in our modern society is to give 'the meaning of crime' to 'more and more of what is seen as unwanted or at least dubious acts', and for 'more and more of these crimes are met with imprisonment'.

One may say that the tendency to reduce the variance with the help of legally defined categories, and the ensuing spatial segregation of difference, is likely to become a must, and certainly grows in demand, once with the advent of modern conditions the physical density of the population tends to become considerably greater than its moral density, and grows much beyond the absorptive capacity of human intimacy and the reaches of the personal-relations network. But one can also reverse the connection and conclude that spatial separation which adds vigour to that reduction is itself a major resource used to prolong and perpetuate that mutual estrangement in which the reductionist operations, also the reductionist impact of criminal law, become a must. The other – cast in a condition of enforced unfamiliarity guarded and cultivated by the closely supervised space boundaries, held at a distance and barred regular or sporadic communicative access – is by the same token kept in his form of the stranger, having been effectively stripped of the individual, personal uniqueness which alone could prevent stereotyping and so outweigh or mitigate the reductionist impact of the law – also the criminal law.

As a (thus far) distant ideal, a total isolation beckons, one that would reduce the other to a pure personification of the punishing force of law. Close to the ideal came American 'state of the art' prisons, like Pelican Bay in California, the state which – to quote Nils Christie's pithy portrayal[3] – 'favours growth and vivacity' and so plans for eight prisoners for every thousand of population by the turn of the century. Pelican Bay prison, according to the enthusiastic report of the *Los Angeles Times* of 1 May 1990, is 'entirely automated and designed so that inmates have virtually no face-to-face contact with guards or other inmates'. Most of the time the inmates spend in 'windowless cells, built of solid blocks of concrete and stainless steel . . . They don't work in prison industries; they don't have access to recreation; they don't mingle with other inmates.' Even the guards 'are locked away in glass-enclosed control booths and communicate with prisoners through a speaker system', and so are seldom, if ever, seen by the prisoners. The sole task left to the guards is to make sure that the prisoners stay locked in their cells – that is they stay non-seeing and non-seen, incommunicado. Apart from the fact that the prisoners are still eating and defecating, their cells could be mistaken for coffins.

At first glance, the Pelican Bay project looks like an updated, state of the art, super-high-tech version of the Panopticon; the ultimate incarnation of Bentham's dream of total control through total surveillance. A second glance reveals, however, the superficiality of the first impression.

Panoptical control had an important function to perform; panoptical institutions were conceived above all as *houses of correction*. The ostensible purpose of correction was to bring the inmates back from the road to moral perdition on which they embarked by their own will or had been pushed for no direct fault of their own; to develop habits which will eventually permit them to return into the fold of 'normal society'; to 'stop the moral rot', to fight back and conquer sloth, ineptitude and disrespect or indifference to social norms – all those afflictions which combined to make the inmates incapable of 'normal life'. Those were the times of the work ethic – when work, hard work and constant work, was seen as simultaneously the recipe for godly, meritorious life and the basic rule of social order. Those were as well the times when the numbers of smallholders and craftsmen unable to make ends meet were growing unstoppably, while the machines which deprived them of a livelihood waited in vain for the compliant and docile hands ready to serve them. And so in practice the idea of correction boiled down to setting the inmates to work – useful work, profitable work. In his vision of the Panopticon Bentham generalized the experience of diffuse yet common efforts to resolve the genuine, irksome and worrying problems confronted by the pioneers of the routine, monotonous, mechanical rhythm of modern industrial labour.

At the time when the project of the Panopticon was sketched, the lack of willing labour was widely seen as the main obstacle to social improvement. The early entrepreneurs bewailed the unwillingness of potential labourers to surrender to the rhythm of the factory labour; 'correction' meant, under the circumstances, overcoming that resistance and making the surrender more plausible.

To sum it up: whatever their other immediate destinations, panoptical-style houses of confinement were first and foremost *factories of disciplined labour*. More often than not, they were also instant solutions to that ultimate task – they set the inmates to work right away, and particularly to the kinds of work least desired by 'free labourers' and least likely to be performed on their own free will, however seductive the promised rewards. Whatever their declared long-term purpose, most panoptical institutions were, right away, *workhouses*.

The designers and promoters of the house of correction founded in Amsterdam in the early seventeenth century, envisaged the production of 'healthy, temperate eaters, used to labour, desirous of holding a good job, capable of standing on their own feet, and God-fearing', and listed a long inventory of manual occupations in which the prospective inmates should engage to develop such qualities – like shoemaking, the manufacture of pocketbooks, gloves and bags, edgings for collars and cloaks, weaving of fustians and worsteds, linen cloth and tapestry, knitting, woodcarving, carpentry, glass blowing, basketry etc. In practice, the productive activity in the house was very soon, after a few half-hearted attempts to follow the initial brief, confined to the rasping of Brazilian logwood, originally named as a means of punishment only – a particularly crude and exhausting labour unlikely to find willing performers if not for the coercive regime of the house of correction.[4]

Whether the houses of correction in any of their many forms ever fulfilled their declared aim of 'rehabilitation', 'moral reform', 'bringing inmates back to social competence', was from the start highly debatable and remains to this day a moot question. The prevailing opinion of researchers is that, contrary to the best of intentions, the conditions endemic to the closely supervised houses of confinement worked *against* 'rehabilitation'. The outspoken precepts of the work ethic do not square with the coercive regime of prisons, under whatever name they appear.

Presenting an opinion that is considered, closely argued and backed by thorough research, Thomas Mathiesen, the eminent Norwegian sociologist of law, declares that 'throughout its history, the prison has actually never rehabilitated people in practice. It has never led to the people's "return to compe-tence".[5] What they did instead was to *prisonize* their inmates (Donald Clemmer's terms)[6] – that is, encourage or force them to absorb and adopt habits and customs typical of the peniten-tiary environment and of such an environment only, and so sharply distinct from the behavioural patterns promoted by the cultural norms ruling in the world outside its walls; 'prisoniza-tion' was the very opposite of 'rehabilitation' and the major obstacle on the 'road back to competence'.

The point is, however, that, unlike in the times when the House of Correction was opened in Amsterdam to the applause of learned opinion, the question of 'rehabilitation' is today prominent less by its contentiousness than by its growing irrelevance. Many criminologists will probably go on for some time yet rehearsing the time-honoured yet never resolved *quer-elles* of penal ideology – but by far the most seminal departure is precisely the abandonment of genuine or duplicitous 'declar-ations of rehabilitating intent' in the contemporary thinking of the practitioners of the penal system.

Efforts to get the inmates back to work may or may not be effective, but they make sense only if work is waiting, and they get their animus from the fact that the work is waiting impatiently. The first condition is today hardly ever met; the second is blatantly absent. Once zealous to absorb ever growing quantities of labour, capital now reacts nervously to the news of falling unemployment; through its stock-exchange plenipoten-tiaries it rewards companies for laying off staff and cutting the number of jobs. Under these conditions, confinement is neither a school for employment nor a second-best, forcible method to augment the ranks of productive labour when the ordinary and preferred 'voluntary' methods fail – to bring into the industrial orbit the particularly reluctant and obstreperous categories of the 'masterless men'. It is rather, under present circumstances, *an alternative to employment*; a way to dispose of, or to neutralize a considerable chunk of the population who are not needed as producers and for whom there is no work 'to be taken back to'.

The pressure today is to *dismantle* the habits of permanent, round-the-clock, steady and regular work; what else may the slogan of 'flexible labour' mean? The strategy commended is to make the labourers *forget*, not to *learn*, whatever the work ethic in the halcyon days of modern industry was meant to teach them. Labour can conceivably become truly 'flexible' only if present and prospective employees lose their trained habits of day-in-day-out work, daily shifts, a permanent workplace and steady workmates' company; only if they do not become habituated to any job, and most certainly only if they abstain from (or are prevented from) developing vocational attitudes to any job currently performed and give up the morbid inclination to fantasize about job-ownership rights and responsibilities.

At their latest annual meeting, held in September 1997 in Hong Kong, the managers of the International Monetary Fund and the World Bank severely criticized German and French methods to get more people back to work. They saw such efforts as going against the grain of 'flexibility of the labour market'. What the latter requires, they said, is the revocation of 'too favourable' job-and-wages-protecting laws, the dismantling of all 'distortions' which stand in the way of unalloyed competitiveness, and breaking the resistance of existing labour to the withdrawal of their acquired 'privileges'[7] – that is, of everything concerned with the stability of their employment and the protection of their jobs and incomes. In other words, what is needed are new conditions which would favour habits and attitudes diametrically opposed to those which the work ethic prophesied, and the panoptical institutions expected to implement that ethic, promoted. Labour must unlearn its hard-trained dedication to work and its hard-won emotional attachment to the workplace as well as the personal involvement in its well-being.

In this context the idea of the Pelican Bay prison as the

continuation of the early industrial workhouses whose experience, ambitions and unresolved problems the project of the
Panopticon reflected, looks much less convincing. No productive work is done inside the concrete walls of Pelican Bay
prison. No training for work is intended either: there is nothing
in the prison's design which may set the stage for such activity.
Indeed, for the convicts Pelican Bay is not a school of anything
– even of purely formal discipline. The whole point of the
Panopticon, the paramount purpose of the constant surveillance, was to make sure that the inmate went through certain
motions, followed certain routine, did certain things. But what
the inmates of the Pelican Bay prison *do* inside their solitary
cells *does not matter*. What *does matter* is that *they stay there*.
Pelican Bay prison has not been designed as a factory of
discipline or disciplined labour. It was designed as a *factory of
exclusion* and of people habituated to their status of the *excluded*.
The mark of the excluded in the era of time/space compression
is *immobility*. What the Pelican Bay prison brings close to
perfection is the technique of *immobilization*.

If the concentration camps served as laboratories of a totalitarian society, where the limits of human submission and
serfdom were explored, and if the Panopticon-style workhouses
served as the laboratories of industrial society, where the limits
of routinization of human action were experimented with – the
Pelican Bay prison is a laboratory of the 'globalized' (or
'planetary', in Alberto Melucci's terms) society, where the
techniques of space-confinement of the rejects and the waste of
globalization are tested and their limits are explored.

Prisons in the post-correction age

Apart from the rehabilitating function, Thomas Mathiesen in
his book *Prison on Trial* scrupulously examines other widely
used assertions meant to justify the use of imprisonment as a

method of resolving acute and noxious social problems – the theories of the preventive role of prisons (in both the universal and individual senses), of incapacitation and deterrence, of simple retribution – only to find them all, without exception, logically flawed and empirically unsustainable. No evidence of any sort has thus far been collected to support, let alone to prove, the assumptions that prisons perform the roles ascribed to them in theory, and that they achieve any degree of success if they try to perform them – while the justice of the most specific measures which such theories propose or imply fail the simplest tests of ethical soundness and propriety. (For instance: 'what is the moral basis for punishing someone, perhaps hard, in order to prevent entirely different people from committing equivalent acts?' The question is all the more ethically worrying for the fact that 'those we punish to a large extent are poor and highly stigmatized people in need of assistance rather than punishment'.)[8]

The numbers of people in prison or awaiting likely prison sentences are growing, and fast, in almost every country. Nearly everywhere the network of prisons enjoys a building boom. State-budget expenditure on the 'forces of law and order', mainly the active police force and prison service, are on the rise throughout the globe. Most importantly, the proportion of population in direct conflict with the law and subject to imprisonment is growing at a pace which signals more than a purely quantitative change and suggests a 'greatly increased significance of the institutional solution as a component in criminal policy' – and signals, moreover, that there is a presumption made by many governments and enjoying wide support of public opinion that 'there is an increased need for disciplining of important population segments and groups'.[9]

What the sharp acceleration of the punishment-by-incarceration suggests, in other words, is that there are some new and large sections of the population targeted for one reason or another as a threat to social order, and that their forcible eviction from social intercourse through imprisonment is seen as an effective method to neutralize the threat or calm the public anxiety which that threat evokes.

The proportion of the population serving prison sentences is different in different countries, reflecting idiosyncrasies of cultural traditions and histories of penal thought and practices, but rapid growth seems to be a universal phenomenon throughout the 'most developed' tip of the world. According to the most recent data meticulously collated by Nils Christie, the USA is notoriously in the lead and far ahead of the rest (though its records are fast approached by the new Russian Federation): altogether, more than 2 per cent of the total population of the USA was under control of the penal law system. The rate of growth is most impressive. In 1979 there were 230 prisoners per 100,000 inhabitants – there were 649 on 1 January 1997. (In some areas, of course, the ratio is much higher: in the district of Anacostia, where most of Washington's poorest population is condensed, half of male residents of the 16–35 age bracket are currently either awaiting trial, already in prison, or on probation.)[10] The USA so far stands alone, but the acceleration of pace is visible almost everywhere. Even in Norway, known to be particularly reticent in resorting to prison sentences, the proportion of prisoners went up from below 40 per 100,000 inhabitants in the early 1960s to 64 per 100,000 now. In Holland the proportion went up from 30 to 86 per 100,000 during the same period; in England and Wales the proportion has now reached 114 prisoners per 100,000 of population and the country 'needs one new prison each week to house the seemingly never ending increase'.[11]

Since the growth is not confined to a selected group of countries but is well-nigh universal, it would be probably misleading – if not downright futile – to seek the explanation in the state-bound policies or the ideologies and practices of this or that political party (even if it would be similarly wrong to deny the modifying impact that such policies may exert on accelerating or slowing down the growth). Besides, there is no evidence that the trust in prison as the principal tool to resolve what has been defined as vexing and anxiety-arousing problems has anywhere become a serious issue in electoral battles; the competing forces, even if miles apart on other hot issues, tend to manifest a complete agreement on this one – and the sole publicly displayed concern of each of them is to convince the electorate that it will be more determined and merciless in pursuing the imprisonment of criminals than its political adversaries. One is tempted to conclude, therefore, that the causes of the discussed growth must be of a supra-party and supra-state nature – indeed, of a global rather than local (in either territorial or cultural sense) character. In all probability, these causes are more than contingently related to the broad spectrum of transformations subsumed under the name of globalization.

One evident cause of the discussed growth is the spectacular promotion of issues classified under the 'law and order' rubric in the panoply of public concerns, particularly as such diffuse concerns are reflected in the learned and authoritative interpretations of social ills and in political programmes promising to repair them. In *Postmodernity and its Discontents* (Polity Press, 1997) I argued that whether Sigmund Freud was right or wrong in suggesting that the trading-off of a considerable part of personal liberty for some measure of collectively guaranteed security was the main cause of psychical afflictions and sufferings in the 'classic' period of modern civilization – today, in the late or postmodern stage of modernity, it is the opposite tendency, the inclination to trade off a lot of security in exchange for removing more and more constraints cramping the exercise of free choice, which generates the widespread sentiments of fear and anxiety. It is these sentiments which seek their outlet (or are being channelled) in the concerns with law and order.

To comprehend fully this remarkable 'transfer of anxiety' one needs to reunite what the language, in its sometimes excessive zeal to divide and circumscribe, has separated. The emotional/

attitudinal unity which underlies the allegedly distinct, since
linguistically set apart, experiences of security, safety and certainty is difficult to detect for the English-speaker, but much
better grasped by speakers of German, thanks to the otherwise
rare frugality of their language: the German word *Sicherheit*
grasps all three experiences (of safety, security and certainty)
and so refuses to accept their mutual autonomy which English
speakers are linguistically trained to take for granted.

If *Freiheit* was made vulnerable by the early modern quest for
the safety, security and certainty of order, *Sicherheit* is the prime
victim of the late-modern career of individual freedom. And
since we would hardly be able to tell apart the three kinds of
unease were it not for the three words that suggest three
semantic objects, there is little wonder that the dearth of risk-
free, that is *secure* choices, and the growing unclarity of the
game-rules which renders *uncertain* most of the moves and even
more the outomes of the moves, tend to rebound as perceptions
of threats to *safety* – first to the body, and then to property, the
body-space extension. In an ever more insecure and uncertain
world the withdrawal into the safe haven of territoriality is an
intense temptation; and so the defence of the territory – the
'safe home' – becomes the pass-key to all doors which one feels
must be locked to stave off the triple threat to spiritual and
material comfort.

A lot of tension accumulates around the quest for safety. And
where there is a tension, political capital will surely be spotted
by bright investors and expedient stock-brokers. Appeals to
safety-related fears are truly supra-class and cross-party, as are
the fears themselves. It is perhaps a happy coincidence for
political operators and hopefuls that the genuine problems of
insecurity and uncertainty have condensed into the anxiety
about safety; politicians can be supposed to be doing something
about the first two just because being seen to be vociferous and
vigorous about the third.

A happy coincidence, indeed, since the first two worries are, in fact, intractable. Governments cannot seriously promise anything but more 'flexibility of labour' – that is, in the ultimate account, more insecurity and ever more painful and incapacitating insecurity. Serious governments cannot promise certainty either; that they must concede freedom to notoriously erratic and unpredictable 'market forces', which, having won their exterritoriality, are far beyond the reach of anything the hopelessly 'local' governments can do, is almost universally taken for a foregone conclusion. Doing something, or being seen to be doing something, about fighting crime threatening personal safety is, however, a realistic option – and one containing a lot of electoral potential. *Sicherheit* will gain little as a result, but the ranks of voters swell.

Safety: a tangible means to an elusive end

Reducing the complex issue of *Sicherheit* to that of personal safety has other political advantages as well. Whatever one may do about safety is incomparably more spectacular, watchable, 'televisable' than any move aimed at the deeper, but – for the same reason – less tangible and apparently more abstract, layers of the malaise. Fighting crime, like crime itself, and particularly the crime targeted on bodies and private property, makes an excellent, exciting, eminently watchable show. The mass media producers and script-writers are well aware of this. If one judged the state of society after its dramatized representations (as most of us do, whether or not we are ready to admit it to others and to ourselves) – not just the proportion of criminals to 'ordinary folk' would appear to exceed by far the proportion of the population already kept in jail, and not only the world as a whole would seem to be divided primarily into criminals and the guardians of order, but the whole of human life would seem to navigate the narrow gorge between the threat of physical assault and fighting back the potential attackers.

The overall effect is the self-propelling of fear. The preoccupation with personal safety, inflated and overloaded with meanings beyond its capacity due to the tributaries of existential insecurity and psychological uncertainty, towers yet higher over all other articulated fears, casting all other reasons of anxiety into yet deeper shade. Governments may feel relieved: no one or almost no one would press them to do something about things which their hands are much too small and feeble to grasp and hold. No one would accuse them either of remaining idle and doing nothing of relevance to human anxieties when watching daily documentaries, dramas, docudramas and carefully staged dramas disguised as documentaries, telling the story of new and improved police weapons, high-tech prison locks and burglar and car-theft alarms, short sharp shocks administered to the criminals, and valiant security officers and detectives risking their lives so that the rest of us may sleep in peace.

Building new prisons, writing up new statutes which multiply the number of breaches of the law punishable with imprisonment, and making the lengthening of sentences mandatory – all these measures increase the popularity of governments; they show the governments to be tough, resourceful and determined, and above all 'doing something', not just, explicitly, about personal safety of its subjects, but by implication about their security and certainty as well; and doing it in a highly dramatic, tangible and visible, and so convincing, fashion.

The spectacularity – the versatility, harshness and promptness – of punitive operations matters more than their effectiveness, which, given the listlessness of public attention and the short life-span of public memory, is seldom tested anyway. It matters more even than the actual volume of detected and reported crimes; though it helps, of course, if time and again a new kind of crime is brought to public attention and found to be particularly odious and repulsive as well as ubiquitous, and if a new detecting/punishing campaign is launched, since this helps to keep the public mind on the dangers rooted in crime and criminals and prevents the public from reflecting on why, despite all that policing promised to bring the coveted *Sicherheit* about, one still feels unsure, lost and frightened as before.

There is more than a happy coincidence between the tendency to conflate the troubles of the endemic insecurity and uncertainty of late-modern/postmodern being in a single, overwhelming concern about personal safety – and the new realities of nation-state politics, and particularly of the cut-down version of state sovereignty characteristic of the 'globalization' era.

To focus locally on the 'safe environment' and everything it may genuinely or putatively entail, is exactly what 'market forces', by now global and so exterritorial, want the nation-state governments to do (effectively barring them from doing anything else). In the world of global finances, state governments are allotted the role of little else than oversized police precincts; the quantity and quality of the policemen on the beat, sweeping the streets clean of beggars, pesterers and pilferers, and the tightness of the jail walls loom large among the factors of 'investors' confidence', and so among the items calculated when the decisions to invest or de-invest are made. To excel in the job of precinct policeman is the best (perhaps the only) thing state government may do to cajole nomadic capital into investing in its subjects' welfare; and so the shortest roads to the economic prosperity of the land, and so hopefully to the 'feel good' sentiments of the electors, lead through the public display of the policing skill and prowess of the state.

The care of the 'orderly state', once a complex and convoluted task, reflecting the multiple ambitions and wide and multi-faceted sovereignty of the state, tends as a result to narrow to the task of fighting crime. In that task, though, an increasingly privileged, indeed a leading role, is allocated to the policy of imprisonment. The centrality of crime-fighting does not by itself explain the prison boom; after all, there are also other ways to fight back the real or alleged threats to citizens' personal safety. Besides, putting more people in jail and for a longer time has not thus far been shown to be the most effective among these ways. One would guess therefore that some other factors favour the choice of prison as the most convincing proof that indeed 'something has been done', that words have flesh and bones. To posit imprisonment as the crucial strategy in the fight for citizens' safety means addressing the issue in a contemporary idiom, using language readily understood and invoking commonly familiar experience.

Today's existence is stretched along the hierarchy of the global and the local, with global freedom of movement signalling social promotion, advancement and success, and immobility exuding the repugnant odour of defeat, failed life and being left behind. Increasingly, globality and locality acquire the character of contrary values (and paramount values at that), values most hotly coveted or resented and placed in the very centre of life dreams, nightmares and struggles. Life ambitions are more often than not expressed in terms of mobility, the free choice of place, travelling, seeing the world; life fears, on the contrary, are talked about in terms of confinement, lack of change, being barred from places which others traverse easily, explore and enjoy. 'The good life' is life on the move; more precisely, the comfort of being confident of the facility with which one can move in case staying on no longer satisfies. Freedom has come to mean above all freedom of choice, and choice has acquired, conspicuously, a spatial dimension.

In the era of time/space compression, so many wonderful and untried sensations beckon from afar, that 'home', though as always attractive, tends to be enjoyed most in the bitter-sweet emotion of homesickness. In its solid, brick-and-mortar embodiment, 'home' breeds resentment and rebellion. If locked from outside, if getting out is a distant prospect or not a feasible prospect at all, the home turns into jail. Enforced immobility, the condition of being tied to a place and not allowed to move elsewhere, seems a most abominable, cruel and repulsive state; it is the prohibition of movement, rather than the frustration of an actually felt wish to move, which renders that condition especially offensive. Being prohibited from moving is a most potent symbol of impotence, incapacitation – and pain.

No wonder, therefore, that the idea of the prison sentence being, simultaneously, the most effective method of disempowering potentially harmful people and a most painful retribution for ill deeds, easily 'makes sense' and altogether 'stands to reason'. Immobilization is the fate which people haunted with the fear of their own immobilization would naturally wish and demand to be visited upon those whom they fear and consider deserving a harsh and cruel punishment. Other forms of deterrence and retribution seem woefully lenient, inadequate and ineffective – painless – by comparison.

Prison, though, means not only immobilization, but eviction as well. This adds further to its popular attraction as the favourite means to 'strike at the roots of danger'. Imprisonment means protracted, perhaps permanent exclusion (with the death penalty offering the ideal pattern by which the length of all other sentences is measured). This meaning also strikes a highly sensitive chord. The slogan is to 'make our streets safe again' – and what else promises better to fulfil this slogan than the removal of the danger-carriers into spaces out of sight and out of touch – spaces they cannot escape?

The ambient insecurity focuses on the fear for personal safety; that in turn sharpens further, on the ambivalent, unpredictable figure of the stranger. Stranger in the street, prowler around the home . . . Burglar alarms, the watched and patrolled neighbourhood, the guarded condominium gates – they all serve the same purpose: keeping the strangers away. Prison is but the most radical among many measures – different from the rest in the assumed degree of effectiveness, not in kind. People brought up in the culture of burglar alarms and anti-theft devices tend to be the natural enthusiasts of prison sentences, and ever longer prison sentences. It all ties together very nicely – logic is restored to the chaos of existence.

The out of order

'Today we know', writes Thomas Mathiesen, 'that the penal system strikes at the "bottom" rather than at the "top" of society.'[12] Why this should be the case has been amply explained by the sociologists of law and practices of punishment. Several causes have been repeatedly discussed.

First among them are the somewhat selective intentions of the lawgivers, concerned with the preservation of a certain specific kind of order. The actions most likely to be committed by people that order has no room for, by the underdog and the downtrodden, stand the best chance of appearing in the criminal code. Robbing whole nations of their resources is called 'promotion of free trade'; robbing whole families and communities of their livelihood is called 'downsizing' or just 'rationalization'. Neither of the two has been ever listed among criminal and punishable deeds.

Moreover, as every police unit dedicated to 'serious crime' will have found out, illegal acts committed at the 'top' are exceedingly difficult to disentangle from the dense network of daily 'ordinary' company dealings. When it comes to activity which openly pursues personal gain at the expense of others, the borderline between moves that are allowed and disallowed is necessarily poorly defined and always contentious – nothing to compare with the comforting unambiguity of the act of safe-breaking of forcing a lock. No wonder that, as Mathiesen finds out, the prisons 'are above all filled by people from the lower strata of the working class who have committed theft and other "traditional" crimes'.

Poorly defined, crimes 'at the top' are in addition awfully difficult to detect. They are perpetrated inside a close circle of people united by mutual complicity, loyalty to the organization and *esprit de corps*, people who usually take effective measures to detect, silence or eliminate potential whistle-blowers. They require a level of legal and financial sophistication virtually impossible to penetrate by outsiders, particularly by lay and untrained outsiders. And they have 'no body', no physical substance; they 'exist' in the ethereal, imaginary space of pure abstraction: they are, literally, *invisible* – it takes an imagination on a par with that of the perpetrators to spy out a substance in the elusive form. Guided by intuition and common sense, the public may well suspect that some theft played its part in the history of fortunes – but to point one's finger at it remains a notoriously daunting task.

Only in rare and extreme cases do 'corporate crimes' come to court and into public view. Embezzlers and tax cheaters have an infinitely greater opportunity for an out-of-court settlement than do pickpockets or burglars. Apart from anything else, the agents of local orders arc all too aware of the superiority of global powers and so consider it a success if they get as far as that.

Furthermore, as far as crimes 'at the top' are concerned the vigilance of the public is at best erratic and sporadic, at worst non-existent. It takes a truly spectacular fraud, a fraud with a 'human touch', where the victims – pensioners or small savers – can be personally named (and even then it takes in addition all the imaginative and persuasive gifts of a small army of popular press journalists) to arouse public attention and keep it aroused for longer than a day or two. What is going on during the trials of high-level fraudsters defies the intellectual abilities of ordinary newspaper-readers and, besides, is abominably short of the drama which makes the trials of simple thieves and murderers such a fascinating spectacle.

Most importantly, though, crime 'at the top' (usually an extraterritorial 'top') may be in the last account a principal or contributing cause of existential insecurity, and so directly relevant to that vexing anxiety which haunts the denizens of late-modern society and makes them so obsessed with personal safety – but by no stretch of imagination can it be conceived of as, of itself, a threat to that safety. Any danger which may be sensed or surmised in crime 'at the top' is of an altogether different order. It would be extremely hard to envisage how bringing the culprits to justice might alleviate the daily sufferings ascribed to the more tangible dangers lurking in the rough districts and mean streets of one's own city. There is, therefore, not much political capital which can be squeezed out of 'being seen to be doing something' about crime 'at the top'. And there is little political pressure on the legislators and guardians of order to strain their minds and flex their muscles in order to make the fight against that kind of crime more effective; no comparison here with the public hue-and-cry against car thieves, muggers or rapists, as well as against all those responsible for law and order who are seen as too lax or lenient in transporting them to prison, where they belong.

Last but not least, there is that tremendous advantage the new global elite enjoys when facing the guardians of order: orders are local, while the elite and the free market laws it obeys are translocal. If the wardens of a local order get too obtrusive and obnoxious, there is always the possibility of appealing to the global laws to change the local concepts of order and the local rules of the game. And of course there is the possibility of moving away if things locally get too hot for comfort; the 'globality' of the elite means mobility, and mobility means the ability to escape and evade. There are always places where local guardians of order are glad and willing to look the other way in case a clash does happen.

All these factors taken together converge on a common effect: the identification of crime with the (always local) 'underclass' – or, which amounts to much the same, the criminalization of poverty. The most common types of criminals in public view come almost without exception from the 'bottom' of society. Urban ghettos and no-go areas are seen as the breeding grounds of crime and criminals. And conversely – sources of criminality (of that criminality which truly counts – one seen as the threat to personal safety) appear to be unambiguously local and localized.

Donald Clemmer coined in 1940 the term 'prisonization' to denote the true effects of confinement, sharply different from the 're-educating' and 'rehabilitating' impact ascribed to imprisonment by its theorists and promoters. Clemmer found inmates being assimilated into a highly idiosyncratic 'prison culture', which – if anything – made them even less fit than before for life outside the prison walls, and less capable of following the rules and usages of 'ordinary' life. Like all cultures, prison culture had a self-perpetuating capacity. Prison was, in Clemmer's opinion, a school of crime.

Fourteen years later Lloyd W. McCorkle and Richard R. Korn published another set of findings,[13] which brought into relief the mechanism making prisons into such schools of crime. The whole police/judicial process culminating in imprisonment is, in a sense, one long and tightly structured ritual of symbolic rejection and physical exclusion. Rejection and exclusion are humiliating and meant to be such; they are meant to result in the rejected/excluded accepting their social imperfection and inferiority. No wonder the victims mount a defence. Rather than meekly accepting their rejection and converting official rejection into self-rejection, they prefer to reject their rejectors.

To do that, the rejected/excluded resort to the sole means at their disposal, which all contain some measure of violence; the sole resource that may increase their 'nuisance power', the only power they can oppose to the overwhelming might of their rejectors/excluders. The strategy of 'rejecting the rejectors' quickly sinks into the stereotype of the rejected, adding to the image of crime the traits of the criminals' inherent proclivity to recidivism. At the end of the day, prisons emerge as the principal tools of a self-fulfilling prophecy.

This does not mean that there are no other causes of crime and no genuine criminals; it means, though, that the rejection/exclusion practised through the prison system is an integral part of the social production of crime, and that its influence cannot be neatly disentangled from the overall statistics of the incidence of criminality. It also means that once prisons have been identified as outlets for mostly lower-class or 'underclass' elements – one would naturally expect the self-confirming and self-perpetuating effects to be at its most emphatic, and so the criminality to be 'most evident', at the 'bottom' reaches of society.

Clemmer and McCorkle & Korn conducted their research among the inmates of prisons and articulated their findings in terms of the effects of imprisonment. One can suppose, though, that what they sought and found was not so much the effects of prison as such, as of the much wider phenomena of *confinement*, *rejection* and *exclusion*. That, in other words, prisons served as laboratories in which trends ubiquitously present (though in a somewhat more diluted form) in 'normal' life could be observed in their most condensed and purified shape (Dick Hebdidge's seminal study *Hiding in the Light* corroborates this guess). If this were correct, then the effect of 'prisonization' and the widespread choice of the strategy of 'rejecting the rejectors', with all its self-propelling capacity, would go a long way towards cracking the mysterious logic of the present-day law-and-order obsession; it would also go towards explaining the apparent success of the stratagem of substituting that obsession for a serious attempt to face the challenge of the accruing existential insecurity.

It may also help to understand why the exemption from global freedoms tends to rebound in the fortification of localities. Rejection prompts the effort to circumscribe localities after the pattern of concentration camps. Rejection of the rejectors prompts the effort to transform the locality into a fortress. The two efforts reinforce each other's effects, and between themselves make sure that fragmentation and estrangement 'at the bottom' remain the twin siblings of globalization 'at the top'.

Notes

Chapter 1 Time and Class

1 See Albert J. Dunlap (with Bob Andelman), *How I saved Bad Companies and Made Good Companies Great* (New York, Time Books, 1996), pp. 199–200.

2 Denis Duclos, 'La cosmocratie, nouvelle classe planétaire', *Le monde diplomatique*, August 1997, p. 14.

3 Alberto Melucci, *The Playing Self: Person and Meaning in the Planetary Society* (Cambridge University Press, 1966), p. 129.

4 See Paul Virilio, 'Un monde surexposé: fin de l'histoire, ou fin de la géographie?', *Le monde diplomatique*, August 1997, p. 17. The idea of the 'end of geography' was first advanced, to my knowledge, by Richard O'Brien (see his *Global Financial Integration: The End of Geography* (London, Chatham House/Pinter, 1992)).

5 Michael Benedikt, 'On Cyberspace and Virtual Reality', in *Man and Information Technology*, (lectures from the 1994 international symposium arranged by the Committee on Man, Technology and Society at the Royal Swedish Academy of Engineering Sciences (IVA) (Stockholm, 1995), p. 41.

6 Timothy W. Luke, 'Identity, Meaning and Globalization: Detraditionalization in Postmodern Space-Time Compression', in *Detraditionalization*, ed. Paul Heelas, Scott Lash and Paul Morris (Oxford, Blackwell, 1996), pp. 123, 125.

7 Paul Virilio, *The Lost Dimension* (New York, Semiotext(e), 1991), p. 13.

8 Margaret Wertheim, 'The Pearly Gates of Cyberspace', in *Archi-*

tecture of Fear, ed. Nan Elin (New York, Princeton Architectural Press, 1997), p. 296.

9   See Steven Flusty, 'Building Paranoia', in *Architecture of Fear*, ed. Nan Elin, pp. 48–9, 51–2.

10   See Dick Hebdige, *Hiding in the Light* (London, Routledge, 1988), p. 18.

11   Gregory Bateson, *Steps to an Ecology of Mind* (Frogmore, Paladin, 1973), pp. 41–2.

12   Nils Christie, 'Civility and State' (unpublished manuscript).

Chapter 2   Space Wars: a Career Report

1   See Edmund Leach, 'Anthropological aspects of language: animal categories and verbal abuse', in *New Directions in the Study of Language*, ed. Eric H. Lenneberg (University of Chicago Press, 1964).

2   Bronisław Baczko, *Utopian Lights: The Evolution of the Idea of Social Progress*, trans. Judith L. Greenberg, (New York, Paragon House, 1989), pp. 219–35.

3   *Histoire des Sévarambes* by D. Veirasse was, according to Baczko, a reading so popular in the century of Enlightenment, that for instance Rousseau and Leibnitz quoted from it without indicating the source, obviously appealing to knowledge common among their readers.

4   See Jürgen Habermas, *The Philosophical Discourse of Modernity* (Cambridge, Mass., MIT Press, 1987), p. 323.

5   The content of *La ville radieuse* has been subjected to a most incisive and inventive analysis by Yale political sociologist Jim Scott; the commentary that follows owes a lot to his seminal insights.

6   Richard Sennett, *Uses of Disorder: Personal Identity and City Life* (London, Faber & Faber, 1996), esp. pp. 39–43, 101–9, 194–5.

7   Nan Elin, 'Shelter from the Storm, or Form Follows Fear and Vice Versa', in *Architecture of Fear*, ed. Nan Elin (New York, Princeton Architectural Press, 1997), pp. 13, 26. The collection of essays *Architecture of Fear* has been inspired by Nan Elin's experience during his field research conducted in the carefully

designed French 'new town' Jouy-le-Moutier. Elin was amazed to find out that 'the subject of fear [*l'insécurité*] arose despite the minuscule crime rate in the area' (p. 7).

8 Mark Poster, 'Database as discourse, or electronic interpellations', in *Detraditionalization*, ed. Paul Heelas, Scott Lash and Paul Morris (Oxford, Blackwell, 1996), pp. 291, 284.

9 See Thomas Mathiesen, 'The viewer society: Michel Foucault's "Panopticon" revisited', *Theoretical Criminology*, (1997), pp. 215–34.

10 George Gerbner and Larry Gross, 'Living with television: the violence profile', in *Journal of Communication*, 26 (1976), pp. 173–98. Quoted in Mathiesen, above.

Chapter 3   After the Nation-state – What?

1 Richard Sennett, 'Something in the city: the spectre of uselessness and the search for a place in the world', *Times Literary Supplement*, 22 September 1995, p. 13.

2 Martin Woollacott, 'Bosses must learn to behave better again', *The Guardian*, 14 June 1997.

3 Vincent Cable, *The World's New Fissures: Identities in Crisis* (London, Demos, 1996), pp. 20, 22.

4 Alberto Melucci, *Challenging Codes: Collective Action in the Information Age* (Cambridge University Press, 1966), p. 150

5 Georg Henrik von Wright, 'The crisis of social science and the withering away of the nation state', *Associations*, 1 (1997), pp. 49–52.

6 Cornelius Castoriadis, 'Pouvoir, politique, autonomie', in *Le monde morcelé* (Paris, Seuil, 1990), p. 124.

7 As might be expected, it is the 'ethnic minorities' or, more generally, small and weak ethnic groups, incapable of running independently a state according to the standards of the 'world of the states' era, which are as a rule most unambiguously enthusiastic about the gathering might of the supra-state formations. Hence the incongruence of claims to statehood argued in terms of allegiance to the institutions whose declared, and even more the suspected, mission is to limit it and in the end to annul it altogether.

8 See Eric Hobsbawm, 'Some reflections on the "break-up of Britain"', *New Left Review*, 105 (1977). Pay attention to the date of this publication: since 1977 the process intuited by Hobsbawm gathered speed and his words are fast becoming flesh.

9 See Cornelius Castoriadis, 'La crise des sociétés occidentales', in *La montée de l'insignifiance* (Paris, Seuil, 1996), pp. 14–15.

10 See 'Sept pièces du puzzle néolibéral: la quatrième guerre mondiale a commencé', *Le monde diplomatique*, August 1997, pp. 4–5. The article is signed 'Sous-Commandant Marcos', and comes from the territory of rural rebellion in Chiapas, Mexico.

11 See René Passet, 'Ces promesses des technologies de l'immatériel', *Le monde diplomatique*, July 1997, p. 26.

12 See Jean-Paul Fitoussi, 'Europe: le commencement d'une aventure', *Le monde*, 29 August 1997.

13 See Claus Offe, *Modernity and the State: East, West* (Cambridge, Polity Press, 1996), pp. vii, ix, 37.

14 See Victor Keegan, 'Highway robbery by the super-rich', *The Guardian*, 22 July 1996.

15 Quoted after Graham Balls and Milly Jenkins, 'Too much for them, not enough for us', *Independent on Sunday*, 21 July 1996.

16 See Ryszard Kapuściński, *Lapidarium III* (Warsaw, 1996).

Chapter 4   Tourists and Vagabonds

1 Michael Benedikt, 'On cyberspace and virtual reality', *Man and Information Technology* (Stockholm, IVA, 1995), p. 42.

2 Ricardo Petrella, 'Une machine infernale', *Le monde diplomatique*, June 1997, p. 17.

3 Jeremy Seabrook, *The Race for Riches: The Human Cost of Wealth* (Basingstoke, Marshall Pickering, 1988), pp. 15, 19.

4 Max Weber, *The Protestant Ethic and the Spirit of Capitalism*, trans. Talcott Parsons (London, George Allen & Unwin, 1976), p. 181.

5 Mark C. Taylor and Esa Saarinen, *Imagologies: Media Philosophy* (London, Routledge, n.d.), Telerotics 11.

6 Agnes Heller, 'Where are we at home?', *Thesis Eleven*, 41 (1995).

7 Jeremy Seabrook, *Landscapes of Poverty* (Oxford, Blackwell, 1985), p. 59.
8 Let us recall that saving the affluent part of Europe from the flood of war refugees was, by the then Secretary of State's admission, the decisive argument in favour of the US involvement in the Bosnian war.
9 See Seabrook, *The Race for Riches*, pp. 163, 164, 168–9.
10 This and later quotations from Jonathan Friedman came from 'Global crises, the struggle for cultural identity and intellectual porkbarrelling: cosmopolitans versus locals, ethnics and nationals in an era of de-hegemonisation', in *Debating Cultural Hybridity*, ed. Pnina Werbner and Tariq Modood (London, Zed Books, 1997), pp. 70–89.
11 See Pierre Bourdieu, 'L'Architecte de l'euro passe aux aveux', *Le monde diplomatique*, September 1997, p. 19.
12 Wojciech J. Burszta, *Czytanie kultury* (Lódź, 1996), pp. 74–5.

Chapter 5   Global Law, Local Orders

1 See Pierre Bourdieu, 'L'architecte de l'euro passe aux aveux', *Le monde diplomatique*, September 1997, p. 19.
2 Nils Christie, 'Civility and State' (unpublished manuscript).
3 Nils Christie, *Crime Control as Industry: towards Gulag, Western Style?* (London, Routledge, 1993), p. 86–7. In the second edition the question mark after the title has been removed.
4 See Thorsten Sellin, *Pioneering in Penology: the Amsterdam Houses of Correction in the Sixteenth and Seventeenth Centuries* (University of Philadelphia Press, 1944), pp. 27–9, 58–9.
5 Thomas Mathiesen, *Prison on Trial: a Critical Assessment* (London, Sage, 1990), p. 40.
6 See Donald Clemmer, *The Prison Community* (New York, Holt, Reinhart & Winston, 1940).
7 See Serge Marti's report from the Hong Kong meeting, 'Le FMI critique les méthodes anti-chômage de Bonn and Paris', *Le monde*, 19 September 1997.
8 Mathiesen, *Prison on Trial*, p. 70.
9 Mathiesen, *Prison on Trial*, p. 13.

10 See Laurent Zucchini, 'Ségrégation ordinaire à Washington', *Le monde*, 25 September 1997.
11 See Nils Christie, 'Penal Geography' (unpublished manuscript).
12 See Mathiesen, *Prison on Trial*, pp. 70–2.
13 See Lloyd W. McCorkle and Richard R. Korn, 'Resocialization within walls', *Annals of the American Academy of Political and Social Science*, 1954, pp. 88–98.

Index